T H E   B R E A K W A T E R   B O O K   O F
CONTEMPORARY NEWFOUNDLAND POETRY

MARK CALLANAN | JAMES LANGER

BREAKWATER BOOKS
P.O. Box 2188, St. John's, NL, Canada, A1C 6E6
WWW.BREAKWATERBOOKS.COM

Copyright © 2013 Mark Callanan & James Langer

LIBRARY AND ARCHIVES CANADA CATALOGUING IN PUBLICATION
The Breakwater book of contemporary Newfoundland
poetry / Mark Callanan, James Langer [editors].
ISBN 978-1-55081-408-8
1. Canadian poetry (English)--Newfoundland and Labrador.
I. Callanan, Mark, 1979- II. Langer, James, 1973-
PS8295.5.N4B74 2013   C811'.60809718   C2013-901009-2

Cover painting: Michael Pittman, *Ignis*, 2008 © CARCC, 2013

We acknowledge the support of the Canada Council for the Arts, which last year invested $154 million to bring the arts to Canadians throughout the country. We acknowledge the Government of Canada through the Canada Book Fund and the Government of Newfoundland and Labrador through the Department of Tourism, Culture and Recreation for our publishing activities.

PRINTED AND BOUND IN CANADA.

Canada Council for the Arts   Conseil des Arts du Canada   Canada   Newfoundland Labrador

Breakwater Books is committed to choosing papers and materials for our books that help to protect our environment. To this end, this book is printed on a recycled paper that is certified by the Forest Stewardship Council®.

CONTENTS

EDITORS' NOTE

For inclusion in this anthology, we have considered any poet who developed—either by birth or residence—a strong relationship with the island of Newfoundland prior to the publication of their first full-length collection of poetry. In cases where a single poem appears in more than one book in an author's oeuvre, we have chosen the latest published version, in deference to the poet's most recent or final vision. While first books are not always represented here, the contributors are arranged chronologically based on the publication dates of their debut collections to better reflect the emergence of individual voices within the context of the island's recent verse tradition.

PROLOGUE

DR. E. J. PRATT, C.M.G. who died in a Toronto hospital on April 26, 1964, at the age of 81, was by far the most considerable of Canadian writers of this century. In his ambition he tried to reflect the greatness of his country, historical and geographical, and his achievement expressed the national genius more finely and richly than ever before. As a Newfoundlander he could be thought of as a recent Canadian citizen, but it was the country as a whole to which he gave his allegiance and took into his scope.

The Times (London), April 28, 1964

AL PITTMAN
1940–2001

THE BORDER

The brook was the border.
We'd gather there on our side
above the falls
on Saturday afternoons
our pockets filled with stones
carefully selected
from the roadside gravel.

They would form up on the far side
and soon the battle would begin.
Rarely did anyone get hurt
but only because our weapons
were inaccurate at such range.
If by chance we did draw blood
we'd jump for joy
all up and down the bank
and the canyon below the falls
would resound with our victory chants.

We never knew them by name
and never cared to.
I don't know why we fought them.
The only thing they had ever done
to us was to return stone-throw
for stone-throw.

Their only offence was
they lived across the brook.

They hated us for the same reason.

BAPTISM

How I should like
to return
to the fields
and lie a while
with new-grown hay
whipping my face
in its breeze-blown
gentle way

And stepping stones
follow a living stream
in winding cataract fashion
down to the sea

And taste the salt
sprayed my way
by shore-crashing waves

And lift my eyes
to the mountains behind
my heart to the sky above

And taste once more
the sweet life
that knows no confession

And is
in itself
a sacrament of the living

COOKS BROOK

At the pool where we used to swim
in Cooks Brook
not everyone had guts enough
to dive from the top ledge

not that it would have been
a difficult dive
except for the shelf of rock
that lay two feet below the surface
and reached quarter of the way out
into the width of the pool

one by one the brave few of us
would climb the cliff to the ledge
and stand poised
ready to plunge headfirst
into the dark water below
and always there was that moment
of terror
when you'd doubt that you could
clear the shelf
knowing full well
it would be better to die
skull smashed open in the water
than it would be to climb
backwards down to the beach

so always there was that moment
when you prayed for wings
then sailed arms outspread into the buoyant air

what you feel is something
impossible to describe
as the water parts like a wound
to engulf you
then closes just as quickly
in a white scar where you entered

and you are surprised always
to find yourself alive
following the streaks of sunlight
that lead you gasping to the surface
where you make your way
leisurely to shore
as though there had been nothing to it
as though it was every day of the week
you daringly defied the demons
who lived so terribly
in the haunted hours of your sleep

HOMECOMING

Carefully, quietly like a thief
I steal toward the bed where you
are sleeping. The serene sound
of your breathing warns me well
you sleep in some sort of peace,
are oblivious to my dark arrival.

Not wanting to wake you out of
whatever warm world you breathe in,
I slide as slow as a glacier into bed,
wrap myself in that most familiar,
most welcome of all the spaces
I so bravely, so cautiously inhabit.

The lovely heat of your hot body
burns me all over in the darkness.
I thrust gently forward and bend
touching my dry mouth to the curve
of your back. Then turn, curled,
to let the night swallow me down.

GRAM GLOVER'S DREAM

from a picture of the same name by David Blackwood

A long thin line
thinner and thinner as it goes
becomes a dot
disappears out where there is nothing

These are the islanders
leaving their island

huddled into the wind
they are going away

out where there is nothing
they have gone away to nothing

the long thin line winds away
in an endless swirl of snow

at the end of the line
turned to the wind
she stands looking back

if she had been farther up the line
she could have been spared this instant

but where she is
at the end of it
she is forced to confront
face to face
the final moment of their going

in a second
when this scene unfreezes
she will turn
become again the last of the line

will turn and walk away
will become nothing in the windy distance

in this instant however
she is frozen where she is

solidified against the wind
she faces the familiar house

on the window a flower pot
and in it a flower bloomed open
to the day's bright light

outside everything is frozen still
everything except the wind

and the wind's white howling

ST. LEONARD'S REVISITED

We came ashore
where wildflower hills
tilted to the tide
and walked
sad and gay
among the turnip cellars
tripping over the cremated
foundations
of long-ago homes
half buried
in the long years' grass

Almost reverently
we walked among the rocks
of the holy church
and worshipped roses
in the dead yard
and came again to the cove
as they did after rosary
in the green and salty days

And men offshore
hauling traps
wondered what ghosts
we were
walking with the forgotten sheep
over the thigh-high grass paths
that led
like trap doors
to a past
they could hardly recall

THE ECHO OF THE AX

My father tells me of the time
he put his hand
on the chopping block
and dared his brother
to cut it off

and whack
just like that
he did it
and my father remembers
the blood on the steel blade
and his mangled hand
hanging barely
by a thread of skin
and he remembers too
how his brother looked
after he'd done it
in that moment
when the whack of the ax
still echoed about the yard

and he recalls
with a heavy breath
how he felt inside
having made his brother
a most amazed victim
of his weird and private fantasies

THE DANDELION KILLERS

for John Steffler

They hate yellow blossoms
and stems whose winged seeds
can clock a lover's fate.

They prefer one shade
and shape of green, grave high,
as level as death.

They crouch in their houses
like soldiers at siege.
Stockpiled in the basement,
a lethal array of weapons.
All their purpose to kill
the colour yellow.

They dwell in panic
and must ever be alert.
The yellow enemy might return,
invade the lawn, thrive again,
spread into the kitchen,
the living room, the bedroom.
The bed.

Imagine having to make love
in a bed full of dandelions.
One hand on your lover's breast,
the other around the throat
of a flower. And not knowing,
night after night, which of you
will be first to touch the agony
of the other's golden death.

BOXING THE COMPASS

The sky is slate grey
threatening rain.
Wind south-southeast.
Maybe more south-by-south-southeast.

The difference could be crucial.

When I was a child
my father took me
around the compass
hundreds and hundreds
of times.

"Boxing the compass" he called it.

Evenings at the kitchen table
he'd draw the compass
on a piece of paper
and have me memorize by name
the thirty-two points from
north to north-north-west-by-north.

We didn't live on the sea then.
And his own ocean-going days
were all long gone.
He drove a car to work.
I walked to school.
The mud-rutted road defined his direction.
The brambled short-cut path defined mine.

But evenings after supper
as though my life depended on it
he'd sit me down beside him

where with a plate from the cupboard
and my school ruler he'd draw
the compass for the thousandth time.

Dusk after dusk
he'd test my memory
until I walked around
inside the house
on the road
in the fields
up the brook
with the compass
spinning this way and that
inside my head.

And sitting in school
through multiplication and long division
through the Ten Commandments and the Beatitudes
through the Crusades and the War of 1812
through the conjugation of latin verbs
through the poems of Bliss Carmen and Pauline
Johnson
I wound around the compass like a clock
gone giddy with turning.

In the middle of his middle age
I bought my father a boat and a compass.
We moored her in the shelter of a small cove
where she could come to no harm
while at rest between her little league voyages
up and down the unhazardous shore.
But even when she was tied up
going nowhere bouncing gently
up and down and around her mooring
I'd see from back aft

my father in the wheelhouse
standing spread-legged.
The wheel in his calloused grip.
His eyes glued to the compass.
And I wondered then
if he was out somewhere
in a bank of fog on the Grand Banks
rolling in a south-east wind
remembering.

Once upon a time
in a fog bank on the Grand Banks
his younger brother went overboard.
And though they searched all night
they couldn't find him.
When the fog lifted at daybreak
they looked again.
But no luck.

My father and my uncle
their brother gone
forever to "the grey seas under"
took their course
and headed south-south-west-by-west
to Boston.

His boat is long gone
to the sand and the seaside grass.
But I still have the compass
he used to navigate his last voyage
to nowhere.
It sits on a stand
in a corner of my living room.
I check it often
each and almost every day.

FINAL FAREWELL

This final farewell
might be as a moth's wings
melting in candle wax.
A reservoir of lava fossilizing
fragments of burnt membrane.
The disintegration of flight.

Or it might be as the death of lilacs
clinging to the end of their own scent
as they go colour-blind out there
on the sunlit, rainswept, windblown tips
of their tombstone twigs.
The grey branches as cold as granite.

Or it might be nothing as neutral
as either of these. The dead-end flight
toward light. The quiet decay of purple.

It may be a denial of death
and downfall. A defiant dedication
to light, flight, bloom, and blossom.
A benediction of being.

Or for the moth, the lilacs, and
for our love, all this may be nothing other
than an end. Where
at the end of things
everything else begins.

ANOTHER NIGHT IN CRAWLEY'S COVE

The accordion considers the tunes it knows best.
The conversation, though incoherent, is congenial.

Outside, the balsams are dancing in the wind.
(The branches, an orchestra of castanets.)
Somewhere in the sky, the birds are sound asleep.

The giddy dancers are stepping it out
on the floorboards of their spindrift dreams.

Tomorrow, the music will be still, the sky quiet
and the birds will be back in the backyard woods.

The day will pass without measure until
night falls and time begins again. The birds
will take to the sky, the dreamers to their feet
and the floor will endure or enjoy another night
of jigs, reels, knee-slapping yarns, out-of-tune
tunes and foot-stomping songs.

Elsewhere in the cove there are people asleep.
They'll be up and about before dawn, long before
the last lie has been told and we've all gone
to rest in peace.

The old Waterford wood stove has grown cold.
Bu there's no discomfort here in this elderly house
on the hill. We are contentedly tired and ready
to creep or crawl to our makeshift beds to await
this day's dawning.

The water, lapping at the landwash, will lull us
to sleep until the birds in the balsams wake us
to another day in Crawley's Cove and another night
close to the floor, well removed from the lives
we live when here is far away. And we are elsewhere.

Where we are the most we have of ourselves.
And the least we have of each other.

TOM DAWE
1940–

BABEL

When the plains were lush
in the lines of after-rain sun,
the engineers were one
in talking of plans for prosperity.
And it came to pass
that their great building towered
into the moving sky.
But there were workers in the basement
who whispered of rumours
that the engineers had argued
on the safety of foundation spans;
and millions of worried faces
flicked up and down in elevators each day
always hurrying and watching clocks
and looking as if somebody
did not understand them;
and there were suicides from top stories
often leaving notes to explain something;
and grumpy janitors pushed big brooms
at the heels of "big shots" working late;
and pretty secretaries frowned
and carried orders from computers
behind closed doors.
Sometimes in the long corridors
children marked messages in crayon
and passing voices wondered
what was "getting into kids today."
And on through miles of night
stretched the on-and-off geometry
of window lights.
And in grey days on the concrete plains
in the oil-lined clouds
the building seemed to lean.

A FAIRY TALE

My great grandmother
is a young girl
lost in the woods.
She carries a berry bucket
and cries
because she has no money
to drive the fairies away.

Watching her,
I am old enough
to be her father.

Her path sinks deeper
into red turf
and bright leaves are sharp.
Old wood has reaching arms
and grey, knobby legs.
Branches are glowing fingers
that cup and cradle the sun.
Faintly, she hears music
on a soft, sap breath
and knows it is not the brook.
Far far away are calling boys
with jam stains on their lips
and laughing girls
clumsy in black, rubber boots
and a clang of dippers.

Just before twilight
she walks out of the woods
and finds a young man fencing
near a crab-apple tree.

He runs to his father
for a horse and cart
and offers her
a ride back home.

On the long way back
through lingering,
still-twig light
they sit close together.
He hums an old love song
learned by some fireside.
The grass is long and green
right up the middle of the road.
Between her knees
she holds her day's berries
like a cask of jewels.

I am patiently waiting
to be born
and wondering
when the cart
will turn into a turnip
or a big red apple on wheels.

I call out to them
as they slide down
gradually
into leafy sunset.
Waving my empty dipper
I run after them.
But they ignore me.
The night closes
around everything.
And strange stars
come out.

OUTPORT CHRISTMAS

Once a year, at least
my mind becomes lined
with yellow paper
from old attic trunks
where sea-gulls glide
in a scent of apples;
cold turkeys recline
on china slabs
in delicious death
as I carry yet
the weight
of a pregnant woolen sock.
I stare through frost glass
holding up a cross;
I watch strange humps of rock
on the eastern snow.
The sock gives birth:
exotic candies
little shepherds
plastic fishes
on an icy morning floor.
I stand
holding the empty skin
under the darkness
of a dead tree
nailed to the roof
yesterday.

ABANDONED OUTPORT

Sun on boarded windows
and gull cries
high in August clouds.

On a small beach-path:
blue-bells nodding
over driftwood.

A bee is buzzing
inside dark cracks
in a window pane.

Clover meadow:
above the rusting ploughshare
a butterfly.

A sudden fog
and sea-winds
bend the sting-nettle.

Deep in graveyard grass
snails and lichens
cling to the headstone.

Across the schoolhouse floor:
paper scraps, dry sea-weed
and a dead moth.

Against the cold twilight:
dark picket-fences
and a crow's flight.

In a rising moon:
a church steeple
and lilac leaves.

EVENING, BARENEED, CONCEPTION BAY

A cold wind
creeps unmarked
through an old picket fence
and eats the salt-stained grass
already dead
on a skull of rock
above the bay
spilling itself
on the teeth
of kelp-ringed crags.

No birds in flight
on a slab of sky.
Beyond
across a bight
a slow mist hangs
in a cross
in a block of window light.

TOP OF THE WORLD

Found this afternoon
at a flea-market:
an old rectangular map
called Top of the World,
just like the one we used
in rough, unready school days,
something free
from a mainland candy factory,
one big-as-life chocolate bar
adorning each corner.
And we in our frosty
hardtack times
were right up there,
bold print declaring it:
the big island of Newfoundland
in top of the world form.
But one day
in the bottom of winter,
a tattered group of us
were punished
for drawing our own
dragons of sorts,
a series of smutty pictures
across the wide, blank spaces
of open sea.
In spirit, we were not
so different really
from old, cautious cartographers
who sketched in sea monsters
as stays against emptiness,

or our methodical ancestors,
who were always in a hobble
about charting their ghosts,
those comforting spirits
so necessary in barren spots
between communities.

EDWARDIANS (OLD PHOTOGRAPH)

For them it is always Sunday afternoon:
six couples in the shade of a tree,
lounging in an English meadow.

They are blurred now:
sepia smokers in straw hats
lolling among wine bottles,
cake-baskets, clover.

They stare out at us:
lotus creatures, insolent somehow
in languid pose,
smug, sprawling, laid-back,
locked there in weekend.

Behind them, over daisy-dotted trench,
a jacket swings carelessly
on a strand of wire
dividing the property,

winding, coiling towards the Channel
perhaps, one inconspicuous,
barbed, metallic cord,
not really symbolic
in this landscape yet.

WILD GEESE

They are passing by, low again,
as they did five summers ago,
their wing beat stirring
the yellow afternoon
of sky and clear pond waters
back through pliant mounds of turf
warm above wave-lilt
over mossy stones.

This was always
my own fishing place
until one day five summers ago
I met him there,
a bent man berry-picking
who said he always thought
this was his secret pond,
but never mind…
I could have it now
as his legs were not
what they used to be.
We sat eating berries
where the brook departed,
watching two wild geese
rise slowly from the lily-pads,
their shadows grazing us
as they turned westward
to fade over distant rampikes.

Today I am watching
the two great birds again
rise up as if a bell
were sounding somewhere
in the partridgeberry hills.
They swing westward
where sky meets marsh leaves,
their shadows almost
touching me.

IF SONNETS WERE IN FASHION

If sonnets were in fashion,
I think I would try one
about a dog I heard
barking one time
in a taped poetry reading
by Robert Frost.
The imagery would be geological
and the old man of fire and ice,
plain diction, the gravel voice
could have the octave
all to himself,
free to be crafty
yet seeming so undesigning
within the confines
of iambic walls,
his presentation glacial, powerful,
moving on the slow import
of its melting....
And then, intruding into line eight,
in a tree-at-my-window pause,
that audible fossil,
just for a couple of seconds,
a dog barking faintly somewhere.

The creature would have the sestet
all to itself,
so perfectly autonomous out there
in pussy-willow swamp
and prime New England sunshine,
casually scanning its territory,
cocking its leg

against the world perhaps,
its primitive spondee
lingering and wonderful.
Oblivious to any
iamb or anapest,
it would just be
its own wild poetry,
a summons
from the wordless places
once again.

ALDERS

Last night I dreamed
they were bringing the world
back,
verdant tongues calling out
to a sun again;
but we were no longer
a part of it.
There had been great snows,
grey rock, and serrated forms
against a sky.
Millions of what we used to
call years had passed
before that
spear of green
between two stones,
that thrust of arrowhead.
Always apprehensive
of their coming,
we had massacred
in the name of clearing,
we who had whittled
small music sometimes
from their supple bones.

Fearful of advance scout,
of any forerunner
of wilderness,
we had always killed
messengers.

BESS

On goat-tramped hills
outside walled towns
in ancient times,
you might have been
the one cast out
to carry plague away.

Further north,
in remote hamlets,
you might have been
village whore, bog-maiden,
noose around neck,
riding rough tumbrel
into oblivion.

In the New World
of Puritans,
you might have been
a scarlet woman
tempting church elders,
labelled by scripture
for prison, stock or scaffold.

For me,
you are a recurring memory
of a trip
to old St. John's.

In a scent of grapes and gasoline
my uncle's loaded drunk,
staggering along.
I'm six years old,
stumbling to keep up,
your raucous voice

calling out to him
through snow squalls
in from the Narrows.

"Sam...Sam...
Ya knows
what I wants now...
me skin."

Suddenly, as you swing from an alley,
he's snarling, cursing,
punching you to the ground.
You crumble like a reefer.

He starts to run
and I run after him,
crying, afraid to look behind.
Pain pricks my ribs.
The wind scrapes
like a splitting-knife.
Drifting snow blurs everything.

So many years ago now,
I still hear him
laughing
on the way home
when I ask
who took your skin away,

poor outport exile,
beaten street-beater,
lady of the flies.

All those winters gone.
A child's question
still jigging in my mind.

NEW YEAR'S MORNING, 2000
for Golda Watts

The world stayed
with us last night.
No aliens danced
on pinpoints in space.
No angels opened books.
No Christ led armies.
The Second Coming
postponed again.
No comets seen.

Just snowflakes this morning,
driven on the wind.
Frost webs, flowers
in window corners.
And, blown off course,
by the last storm
of the millennium,
one small bull bird
tangled in a thorn bush.

Cradling it carefully
in a towel,
we took it back
down the beach road
to find its grooves
again
on the biting wind.

And, on the way back,
stumbling toward us,
as if a scarecrow
had slipped from its cross,
a man in ragged pyjamas
trying to flee
from a nursing home.
Some poor fellow,
not quite making it,
captured,
wrapped in a blanket
by white-coated people
in a van.

THE LAST HOUSE

According to legend,
a bird fluttered
into the great hall
of feasting one night,
above all the music and chatter,
window to window—
then was gone.
And the harpist looked up, singing
our life is like that,
one brief, bright moment
between two darknesses.

This morning I am alone
on the abandoned island,
in the last house standing.
The fires are out,
the music gone.
The feasters have left the table.

I followed something
up from landwash,
small, ruffled, grey,
flitting in through a warped
doorframe,
out another.

In from buttercups
and rat-tails
strumming
on the wind.

Out into sea light
and strings of morning glories
tuned along cellar stones.

JOHN STEFFLER
1947–

TOWERS AND MONUMENTS

three hundred years
and what's there to show?

earthquakes are not the problem, but the sea
always quakes more than the earth ever has
and we live on its edge

balancing
boats on the waves
homes on the shrugging rock

the framing we build spans shore and grey horizon
every day, but the sea slides after us
erasing what we've done

the towers, the monuments you miss are *there*
in the space between ocean and heaven,
we trace them, conjure them out of bustling air
in our songs and stories, we hold them
wild again on the crest of the running instant
and let them go,
back to our dead and the faint days

with nothing to show

from *THE GREY ISLANDS*

Night on the island is full of power. In the dark the land and sea are released from the spell of logic and industry the sun's light places upon them. The water, the trees and hills rise up. They roam and assume what shapes they wish.

At one point last night I stepped out of the cabin and was startled by the gigantic glaring presence of the moon, its reflection reaching in a broad flashing path down the sea, like a river of cold light falling straight to the cabin door. I had never seen the moon so large or so white, and its light seemed too sharp, too keen and alert: as if grinning—not hungrily exactly—but with knowing, exultant power, like some great animal.

It moved briskly, this creature of light, rippling its body with easy energy. And I stood swallowed up, gazing into it. But I could not bear it for long. It was too massive and too cold to confront alone. In a rush I turned back to the cabin and opened the door: the relief! the lantern throwing its cone of warm light over the table, my book, the woodstove crackling contentedly.

from *THE GREY ISLANDS*

Under everything I'm often vaguely anxious, uneasy in the
middle of my actions here. So many things strange to me.
The tide for example. It constantly changes the terrain in the
low shoreland east of the cabin, and I'm always a bit afraid of
getting stranded there.

Paths appear and become submerged. Little knolls that I
cross on foot at one time of the day and fix in my memory as
landmarks, at another time of the day have turned to islands.

At low tide the sea is bordered by natural meadows. The
incoming tide slides up into these grassy fields—a beautiful
lush sight—but tricky as far as walking is concerned. It's
often impossible to know before stepping forward into the
tall grass whether my foot will find solid earth or water
below the leaves—and if there is water, how deep it will be.

CEDAR COVE

If your wharf is washed away
it will come to Cedar Cove—
Wild Cove on the maps or
Capelin Cove. If your boat

goes down it will sail to Cedar
Cove piece by piece.
And your uncle, should he not come back
from his walk on Cape St. George,

will be found grinning among
the glitter of barkless roots
laths struts stays
stringers and frayed rope

in Cedar Cove, where no
cedars have ever grown,
but that's what the local people
call it. The water horizon

topples straight down
on Cedar Cove over
and over, box cars
falling, loads of TNT.

And the wind will not let you speak
in Cedar Cove, which could
be called Deaf Cove
or Lobotomy Cove, will not

let you think or stand straight;
the shrunk trees writhe
and have the wrong kinds
of leaves, but their roots spread

wide in Cedar Cove,
whose gravel is soft compared
to its air. We have come to Cedar
Cove overland, my love

and I, having been lost
at sea in another way.
All day we scatter
ourselves through the noise

and whiteness, learning the thousand
ways things can be taken
apart and reassigned—
the boot sole impaled on the shattered

trunk, the rust flakes,
the bone flakes encrusting a bracelet
of kelp—losing our pictures
of home, stick by stick.

After Cedar Cove,
what will be left of us?

FOR MY EXECUTION

For my execution,
the spot I choose is just to the south
of where the barn used to stand, a zone
where the grass rippled and posed like a handsome animal,
sleek on a century of barnyard loam,

where our horse, Pat, lay down one Saturday morning
and I sat on his flank grinning and squinting into the
east to have my picture taken
and he didn't care,

my sister, housecoated, holding the camera, her neck
and shoulders bitten away by the sun, the milk-house
beside her with its unused well under
a clutter of planks,
the fieldstone throat I would peer down, into
the past, watching a pebble fall—once in a drought,
to water the garden, my father pumped out its
stench, its corpses, liquid blots of fur—

a spot I wanted only to leave,
the cedar rail paddock we built in a bad
mood, the tramped grass steamy as seaweed in the migraine
of noon, lending myself like a slave as we
dug the holes,
postponing my ownership,
reserving my willingness
for my own life, somewhere over the rim of that ploughed
green bowl.

I will kneel and wait for it,
facing east.

THAT NIGHT WE WERE RAVENOUS

Driving from Stephenville in the late October
dusk—the road swooping and disappearing ahead
like an owl, the hills no longer playing dead
the way they do in the daytime, but sticking their black
blurry arses up in the drizzle and shaking themselves,
heaving themselves up for another night of
leapfrog and Sumo ballet—some

trees detached themselves from the shaggy
shoulder and stepped in front of the car. I swerved

through a grove of legs startled by pavement, maybe a
hunchbacked horse with goitre, maybe a team of beavers
trying to operate stilts: it was the

landscape doing a moose, a cow
moose,
most improbable forest device. She danced
over the roof of our car in moccasins.

She had burst from the zoo of our dreams and was
there, like a yanked-out tooth the dentist
puts in your hand.

She flickered on and off.
She was strong as the Bible and as full of lives.
Her eyes were like Halley's Comet, like factory whistles,
like bargain hunters, like shy kids.

No man had touched her or given her movements geometry.

She surfaced in front of us like a coelacanth, like a face
in a dark lagoon. She made us feel blessed.

She made us talk like a cage of canaries.

She reminded us. She was the ocean wearing a fur suit.

She had never eaten from a dish.
She knew nothing of corners or doorways.

She was our deaths come briefly forward to say hello.

She was completely undressed.

She was more part of the forest than any tree.
She was made of trees. The beauty of her face was bred
in the kingdom of rocks.

I had seen her long ago in the Dunlap Observatory.

She leapt from peak to peak like events in a ballad.

She was as insubstantial as smoke.

She was a mother wearing a brown sweater opening her arms.

She was a drunk logger on Yonge Street.

She was the Prime Minister. She had granted us a tiny reserve.

She could remember a glacier where she was standing.

She was a plot of earth shaped like the island of
Newfoundland and able to fly, spring down in the middle of
cities scattering traffic, ride elevators, press pop-eyed
executives to the wall.

She was charged with the power of Churchill Falls.

She was a high-explosive bomb loaded with bones and meat. She broke the sod in our heads like a plough parting the earth's black lips.

She pulled our zippers down.

She was a spirit.

She was Newfoundland held in a dam. If we had touched her, she would've burst through our windshield in a wall of blood.

That night we were ravenous. We talked, gulping, waving our forks. We entered one another like animals entering woods.

That night we slept deeper than ever.

Our dreams bounded after her like excited hounds.

BEYOND NAMES AND LAWS

On Jackson Island Jim snared a rabbit,
skinned it, and worked a half-pound hook
up through its bare muscled ass, its rib cage
and throat, until the barbed tip lodged
in back of its eyes, then tied the hook to a line
as thick as Huck's thumb and let it trail
in the river's pull all night from their raft
moored among willow boughs,

                         and in the morning
hauled what he first took for a sunk stump,
its streaming roots the snaky beard of the biggest
catfish they'd ever seen. It was dead on the line.
They couldn't lift it. They would have towed the monster
to town and sold it and been talked about for years,
if they hadn't been on the run. Made one white
notch in its mossy back, enough for their morning
meal, then cut the line to let the dark
thing roll on ahead of them.

AMORGOS

The way my shadow jolts down the causeway ahead
of me under the street lights—crickets luxurious
in the hot night, in the tough dust-abused shrubs,
the harbour swaying in bright molten vinyls—
tells me I'm drunk. Stick man alone. Talked
for a while with a big-mustached café owner who
was born in Paleokastro on Crete, mentioned
Vai and Sitia, the palm grove, the tourist
bungalows now, as though I'm an old testosterone
lord myself, such shit, even in beauty's beauty
it's possible not to know one word in the language
of sea smell, the language of evening over an
island port, the world made of ripe fruit colours,
petting and aroused sighs, and it's possible
to be lumbering, lead-booted, mute, while
everyone else sees a living mirror that,
when they touch it, has a hand reaching from
inside, belonging to someone who is them and not
them. Place-embraced, wanted, gathered in.

BEATING THE BOUNDS

When I was six years old, my parents,
along with other adults who'd never spoken
to me, came laughing and acting silly,
picking me up, giggling, "Now we'll show
you a house you didn't know about."
"A big house."
"A secret house you knew about all the time."
So I was frightened, seeing how serious
it was that they were so strange,
although I was probably smiling,
and they carried me and other children my age
to the river and said, "Here is the marble
floor," and put my bare legs in the fast
place between stones and it was colder
than I remembered it and the tugging of dark
cold water became my legs, the Fox Island
River became my legs—afterwards when I
was falling asleep or sometimes just walking
along, the bottom of me would be moving away
like that—and they carried me, tickling me,
singing ridiculous songs among rough
brown stones up a valley past caribou
where it was cold and held me up on top
of their palms so I faced the sky and someone
with fat fingers that smelled of sheep held
my eyes open until the cold air and white
sky burned and were too bright and my eyes
brimmed like two cuts and I felt those cuts
go right into my name and they said,
"This is the roof up here, you can't go
higher than this," and that wind and sky
were my eyes then, they were in my name,

and the people pushed me through a patch
of alders and a patch of spruce the wind
had bent, saying, "Here's a young cub
we'll take home and raise," and "Push him in front
so we won't get scratched," and my skin
was crisscrossed with cuts, so I felt
those branches, smelled the alder musk,
the sharp edge of spruce like a coast,
a burning fringe, a noise around me holding
me in and they said, "This is the west
wall of the house you live in, remember
it," and the day went on like that, they
pushed me against a cliff to the north
so I felt its jaggedness in my spine,
they sat me in black soupy peat and said,
"Here is your bed, it is nighttime," they
took me down to the sea and made me
drink it and told me that was the south
and the kitchen, "the garden," someone
laughed and gave me a capelin to eat, rubbed
scales on my face, the backs of my hands
and "Over there," they said, meaning
over the hills across the gulf, "that is not
your house and the people who live there
are strangers to you, not enemies if
you deal with them properly." "They
speak a language of farts," someone said,
"they gobble like turkeys when they fuck,"
and although my body was made of all
it had touched that day and my ears were full
of my parents' voices and the voices
of their friends, in my heart I was still
frightened and felt like a stranger among them.

DIVIDING ISLAND

When they came to the island,
she was pregnant, walked with him
slow, serene each afternoon
down East Valley for raisin pie
at the Seven Seas, lay on a lawn chair
in the empty living room reading.
Then they were three.
He had bargained to keep her
with his work, left his boy self
back in Toronto, laid out a dream
and would make a family, then
they were four, busy around
themselves, noise of themselves,
leaves unfolding, but shivered
to look beyond, greys and blacks
arranged into landscape,
snow in June, in October, proud
of their isolation, the hard
fisherman's history they'd borrowed,
but hating their dislocated selves,
their forced selves, longing to get
back to farmland, cities, unable
to give themselves to the island,
but giving themselves all the same,
keeping shrines to themselves, self-
effigies in the air above them while
they walked muddy Church Street
to the post office, watched their neighbour
chop down the roadside trees
for fuel, grief like a new seed
inside their happiness waiting
its turn, the building, then

the building's emptiness,
the scattering, that to be lived
through too, ache of a landscape
people have always had to leave,
divided from one another to grow,
to get work, hating the newness
where they went, the small picking
insistence of home, homesick,
homeless, the island growing this
history of loss like its low trees,
self-cancelling thoughts, love,
don't love, am, am not, everything
breaking down here, many small
separate parts with wind ruffling
their edges, people split and
split and finally unable to be
anything but the place, speaking
the place, if not joyously
at least beyond care

MARY DALTON
1950–

BRIDESBOYS

Sudden as a northeasterly,
The engagement.
Up and down the harbour, the six of us,
Bidding the neighbours, *come to the wedding*.
Now, we come up with moonshine galore—
Oh yes, more than we bargained for—
My son, we all had a fine jag on.
A racket out on the bridge—
Up she went like a brindy bough,
And the father, stiff as brewis,
Come out and drove us off out of it,
And the water barrels upsot, the
Bride cake made away with.
The day after, a big kick-up.
We were all mops and brooms.
Small chance he'll have us in for a
Bite of the groaning cake
Come the fall.

THE CROSS-HANDED BED

She was a bit of a woman—
A waist like a wasp when I married her,
But strong—no one could beat her for work—
Six loaves every day and the
Wash out on the line
Before the sun rose on the water.
She sang like the wren.
Up at the window when our boat came in.
She welcomed
Each youngster that came,
But the ninth tore her open—
Now she's in the ground
Our old four-poster's all reefs and sunkers
And I'm bound out for Wareham's
In search of a cross-handed bed.

THE DOCTOR

November and a snarling gale.
Out they came in the small hours—
Two red little moon men—
Not the weight of a bag of flour
Between the pair of them. The doctor
Came after the mid-wife, eyed them both,
Barked out his verdict:
Nothing to be done for them,
Was off in a flash. So they
Jammed the stove with junks to the damper,
Stuffed wool from the sheep in a
Drawer from the bureau,
Lined that nest with thick flannel,
Fed them like sick lambs with a dropper.
Six long months they captained
That kitchen, steered those
Two little moon men to shore.

DOWN THE BAY

for J.E.B.

It's so barren down there
A crow's got to bring
A stick to pitch on.

FIRST BOAT

Eyes like the cornflower. And a
Real devil-ma-click—
I knew when I married him.
First boat on the water—
"Where's that sun to,
Lollygagging about?" he'd grin
On his way out the door.
Ours the highest woodstack.
Ours the stable stuffed with hay.
Our goats the fattest.
Our quilts the most rumpled.
He'd ruffle my hair,
Grin, "Where's that sun to,
Lollygagging about?"
Our sweat on his shoulders.
His blue eyes blazing.

JANNEYING

Every winter it was the same racket.
A hint of the janneying, our mother'd
Have copper kittens, but after a bit
She'd give in to us, say yes we could go.
We'd rig ourselves up in any old fit-out,
Pillows and nets, cotton drawers on our heads.
The boys let out squeaks, the girls spoke all gruff—
One fellow missing a finger made up a
False one so he couldn't be guessed.
Once we'd get in, we'd kick up the mats,
Fire up the accordion, dance the whole night—
The floor-boards'd shiver, the funnel turn red.
First light of the sun, off we'd head home,
Bellies rumbling and we ready
To eat the leg off the Lamb of God.

MERRYBEGOT

When the moon was newing and the night burnt black,
Some rapscallion, some young pelt, some nuzzle-tripe
Set off down the path with the go of a born-again preacher,
Crept in under our apple tree, shinnied on up,
Swift and hungry as a starved mosquito, stripped
It bare.
And himself playing Don Juan in the kitchen—
Not a sound did he hear—
No apples for winter
And from the look of her belly
A good chance of a merrybegot.

THE RAGGED JACKET

He'd pinch a quarter till it squeaked—
He'd begrudge the very breath you took.
Might as well try to get blood from a turnip
As ask him for the loan of a copper—
That was the word all over the harbour.
Now he's caught up with that shady outfit;
Now he's the one in the ragged jacket.
Now it's all one to him
That the grave's got no silver sock,
That the shroud's got no pockets.

WINTER COAL

They trotted right up to the foot of the lane,
Cart piled with coal for the light-keeper's shack.
But the cousins said no, no crossing their land—
So they turned round the horse and headed on back
For the boat, loaded her up for the Point.
Jam-packed to the gunnels, she rode low in the water.
A stiff wind from the west and over she went—
Over she toppled, tossed them out in dark water.
One of them got fast to the boat,
Held six hours to the side of her,
His fingernails tore off of him;
His brother's luck broke—
She flipped him in first
And the coal down on top of him.

YET

Moll doll his chin;
Her hair birch-
Broom-in-the-fits;
Chalk and cheese, they said;
Cradle and grave,
They said;
Yet—
You could smell
The smouldering, sparry,
Whenever they met.

SALAX

The salt book is a penance—
I drop it on a kitchen chair.
No salt for the priests of Egypt:
it planted desire, a worm in the belly.
For the tribesmen of Borneo,
bloody after slicing the head from the body,
no sex and no salt.
For the Pima, Apache-killer—and for his wife—
days and days of no sex and no salt.
The sacred whores, wives of the snake-god,
the Nagin women of Behar,
bore their fasts bravely: no sex and no salt.
Begging, they gleaned
gold coins for the priests,
salt and sweets for the people.
For him when he walks down my lane:
black olives, smoked mussels,
brandade, bacalao,
dripless candles, well-salted,
sheets silky—shared salting.

THE SALT MAN

after Mark Kurlansky

It was the depth of winter: musing on small fires,
they found him in the salt-work,
flattened like a codfish in the Dürnberg mountain.
(Two weeks before, a comet-star had shocked their sky.)
Weird one, split cod of a man, a figure out of some
ancient bestiary, cured to a sere yellow-brown,
all the flexed muscle, the running juice of him
pressed down by the mountain of salt.
Yet he was his own salt comet, that newly mined Celt:
resplendent in his twill jacket of roaring red plaid,
his cone-shaped hat, his grand shoes of leather,
his torch of pine sticks lavished with resin,
his horn.
Did his brilliance astonish when he blazed up
sixty-three shoe-lengths and two storied millennia
into the punishing air?

OSMOTIC

The old house is porous. A thick skin
against blows of wind, rain and snow—
against cancerous rays of the sun—
yet for the hill it's osmotic,
opens itself up in small places;
gives access to spider and snail, to
Daddylonglegs, the thin juggler;
lets in ladybug and carpenter cow;
warms up mice fleeing the chill of October,
the skittering ones on the planks overhead.
The house, liminal: at night in her sleeping
it breathes in, breathes out, half in love with
the Other, with salt wind and water.
The maned sweep of waves crashing
up over the Island Rock; the wind barrelling
down from the harbour, out to the Point;
the moon making silver out in the Ram's Horn Bight—
all surge into her sleeping.
She is at one
with the porous house, at ease there
where inner and outer pass freely.

Spantickles flit in the old man's beard.
Pines sprout roses. Sleet needles pucker
the broad beam of the lighthouse.
Ghosts throng the road and bread
is left out for the fairies.
On the sea, wheels of fire and
underneath boats sunken and softening.
A bull with arms builds a house

the colour of money. For sepia
drawings the squid gives its ink:
the lost houses of Gasters,
ruts of the Goat Shore.

Doors give onto doors,
fling themselves wide
in the night-mind,
in the house porous and rooted.

THE BOAT

It was quite the rigamarole—
first the report of the broken boat
found high and dry in a bed of petunias,
then the tale of how it had sailed down
out of the heavens on a cold rainy Tuesday—
out of the great galvanized bucket of the heaving sky—
each of us knew what to make of it.
The mayor proposed a stern letter be written;
the councillor shuffled her ordinances.
The police dogs searched it for drugs.
The priest prayed for the drowned crew.
The biologist listed the worms and the sea-lice.
The woodcarver filled out some forms for the planks.
The camera man assembled his sepia filters.
The psychologist warned of a wave of hysteria.
The evangelist read signs of the pending apocalypse.
The love-sick boy notched *her* name in the hull.
The real-estate agent cooked up a deal.
The historian ransacked his files for parallels.
The artist dreamt of a cottage conversion;
the politician sized up the tourist potential.
The carpenter said it was a big job to fix her;
the hardware men boxed up all sizes of nails.
The poet tossed off an exquisite ode;
the adman was sure he could mount a campaign.
Axe in hand, the fire chief rose to the occasion.
The pigeons were glad of a new perch.
It was quite the ballyhoo. Then,
while they were arguing among themselves
the boat lifted itself up out of their element,
into the blue—its battered planks clattering,
its twisted keel an inward grin—
and moved crazily on.

CARMELITA MCGRATH

1960–

TOURING THE MANOR HOUSES

Excuse me, but I'd rather not see
another broad room
where stippled light
released through leaves reveals
the desk where he wrote that famous tract on natural history,
or that table where he pinned his creatures
and, watching the sky,
ordered the harvest begun.

Not again—please—
her garden room
where her hat hangs
in replica, where she sighed for the apple blossoms,
not her parlour
where her ghost still sits on the green divan,
warming its ankles by the fire.

Show me instead the kitchen,
the distance from the pump,
the slop buckets, the vessels of disposal,
the flatirons,
show me that low stone room where the laundry was done,
the sheets boiled, the pots where hares were simmered,
the small white attic rooms
where the women whose features I bear
unpinned their hair with reddened hands
and dreamt of lovers
coming to them over fields
of August hay.

LOVE AND THE SWAN

It was a year when possibilities
of love were splitting, flying out,
particular, in all directions.

"Do you think it's possible to be in love
with two people at once?" he asked.
"This is not love," I said, sure
under the black June sky, not
a star in sight, the rain's
first whispering pish on the ivy leaves
as if a ghost were brushing against the wall
to eavesdrop on some earthly foolishness.

"And that's not love either," I said, speaking
of the other one, the one of two,
his letter folded like origami in my pocket.
"You. Him. You only want to know
where I am all the time."

Romance had worn off me
or been absorbed like old makeup
that day in Stratford-upon-Avon
when I bent to photograph
the question-mark neck, wings like Gabriel's:
my back was stiff from listening half the night.

When the swan attacked, I smelled
bracken in its feet, old weather and decay
in the pockets of its wings
that beat my head;

the photograph is a blur:
a ripple in a pond,
an echo in it of the harsh voice of the swan
dropping a warning in my ear.
Christ, it was a hard year.

ADAM AND EVE ON A WINTER AFTERNOON

Adam comes in from sawing wood
with a chip on his shoulder.
And grunts. And heaves the wood down,
a heavy drop filled with creeping, unsaid things,
to the woodbox.

And Eve is trying to imagine it not there,
that slow and trembling thing within his breath
that lives between inhale and exhale. This
must be just exertion, and yet it feels
like a weapon, not quite secret but concealed.

She has words for such days—*wood hyacinth,*
aurora borealis, Harley-Davidson—either
ethereal beauty or a fast-flying escape.
But the kitchen is a trap baited with supper cooking
and the imminent arrival of children.

And Adam says, "Whas for supper?"
And Eve says, "Soup."
And he says, "Any meat in it?
I hope you're not off meat again. Growing
children need their protein. And this
is no climate to be eating like rabbits."

And then the old clock rescued from a house
where pouncing bargain hunters drove deals at a death sale
hammers four o'clock home.

And Eve thinks that four o'clocks are old-fashioned flowers,
and she stirs the soup and plunks down
in her bentwood rocker with her seed catalogues,
thinks *crocosmia*
thinks *branching tulip*
thinks *Apricot Beauty*
thinks *hemerocallis*

And the ragged thing between breath and breath
is there again, just for a second, a thing of air
with claws and teeth.

And Adam goes out for another load
before the early dark sinks in on him,
and while his saw buzzes
the language of massacre on wood
thinks *tomorrow's Friday*
thinks *pint of Guinness*
thinks *at least she dyed her hair*
thinks *I can hear the children*

Their footsteps saw over frozen grass, their voices
high, inadvertently calling everything back together,
one of them playing a blackbird's call on a recorder.

AN IDEA OF ORDER IN BEACON HILL PARK

the seagull doesn't like to be ignored, fans
out a white demi-bloom of tail, flies
breast to breast with the water gull below,
a show of sudden flight and reflected shadow

close or at a distance any eye that pans
this wake of flight is led to spaces
in trees where living branch meets dead;
below, spent cigarettes and blossoms, floating birdshit
and feathers where the willow trails its swimmer's hair

these things are not what we've come for—what's advertised
are peacocks, the more iridescently bright the better,
rhododendrons fuschia and puff-sleeved as bridesmaids
in procession and attended by fern fronds

more startling still, a short walk down the street—
ladies and gentlemen—scarlet ibis and flamingoes
under glass. In the land of the newlywed and nearly dead
everything's arranged to please us

but not this misfit, this beautiful fan-tailed scavenger
who, more like us, eats garbage, makes from it ivory plumage,
tries to take over the world, calls out a raucous screed
on the subject of attention here where we've come to scavenge
an idea of the garden, cultivated in empire's detritus

ah look, a lone duckling, an ageing romantic
clucks at the loss of mother but her man looks at his watch,
holds her elbow in a slingshot grip, says
don't worry, honey, it's nature

and along the groomed trails we shuffle out, leave spaces so our tribes
don't meet in unmediated ways until we reach the street
the lights, the flashing crosswalk man we've made
and technobirdsong that must be obeyed

frozen in the sudden open glare, the man
picks a fallen petal from his love's hair,
the signals change, and we walk on in unison
sprouting shreds of blown down and errant pollen.

HEARTS OF PALM

Afternoon, desultory in the aisles
the way one moves distracted in a dream
I spy her sculpted in the white-green light,
a tiny woman in a camel coat, the years worn off it
here and there. Gloved hand outstretched
to roam among the wares
of this attenuated aisle of imports
where not much from anywhere's filtered in.
Tea? I think, as wool-clad fingers flit,
a pale five-winged moth over blackcurrant jam;
a picnic's conjured by the lemon biscuits
until she alights on hearts of palm. A dust-
furred tin. Who knows what dinners
she dreams up, or what is caught in some synaptic clasp,
those night-long dinner parties of the past,
seeing the guests off down ice-slick roads
and lying there in the snowplow-thickened night,
a blue light beating through bare trees
and all the ambient noises of the night
astir in her as birds of wakefulness.
Did she value his body most at times like this
when lost in sculpted sleep he seemed more whole
in his nakedness, more than himself?
Her fingers nesting on his chest,
his captured heart beating through her palm.

BOOMAN

Beware the shadowy booman in the evening garden,
a spectre from the years the grass grew high
as houses. Beware the moment when light is unsure.
There he'll wait,
all smoke and shadow and shimmer-shape.
With the crook of his finger, he'll beckon you over,
'cross the crimped summer hay he'll call you, say
"My, you're after getting some nice fat legs.
My, what a grand big girl."
Once he appeared in a cellar door;
he was not there a second before.
His face wavered in the heat haze
and it was not night, but the burnished
centre of an August day.
I caught his gaze upon my scrawny shape
like a small, chill wind from nowhere,
rising and teasing and falling,
all in a moment, and gone.
The booman waited, found me late
at night on a city street
where trees were thick and crowds thin,
tried to frig me, frighten me
but I got away with loud curses,
the pump of my grand girl's legs. I still expect him
some nights on some streets
where the dark lies heavy and sweet and deep
as the grass where I first found him.
The best protection is to never discount him.

BEFORE ELECTRICITY,
DEMONS WERE A REGULAR OCCURRENCE

The devil, for instance, hid on the gutpath.
Not content to steal young girls at dances
and waste them
or waylay priests on deserted roads,
he frightened fishermen.
You would have thought he worked
for some anti-union interests.
In the blackest night, they'd rise,
the rattle of their lunch cans
filling lanes, summoning dawn.
The devil waited for them:
   horns sharp as steel
   horns black and fiery
   cloven hoofs to trip them up
   body huge and hard to block their way
   beastly snuffle some heard as hellish words.
Better make your sign of the cross
before you near the dock, skipper,
before you cross that stretch of road—
One night, after experiments with wires,
a string of lights white and amber shone
and right above the devil there was one
illuminating a bovine face, wicked horns,
black bull's body sprawled in the gutpath dust.

MY FATHER'S GHOST

My father's ghost, while my father still lived,
haunted a corner of Bond and Bannerman,
and each time I walked by I bit my tongue
to not ask him
"Now what are you doing in town, you never called me?"
Instead as the figure
tipped his peaked cap
and waved a hand that always
held a cigarette, I smiled
"Good day, sir," as I'd been taught
in childhood's other lifetime.
And he responded with comments on the weather.
My father was falling off the slippery slope of earth.
Each day the summoning phone call
hung like a phantom in the air,
already there but waiting to manifest itself.
I imagined conversations with the man
in the peaked cap
that would recall summers of boats laden
with fish and sunlight,
and all the busy men in peaked caps
muscled and brown from splitting cod
and hauling hayloads. He was the last of them,
exhaling the past, all the failing memories
I wanted to draw from him
and carry to my father's body
in a gift of language.
My father's ghost, while my father still lived,
haunted a corner of Bond and Bannerman
and held the better part of a century inside him.
But he was frail and I fearful too long,
returned in grief for the elixir of his memories
to find him gone.

HOW DIFFICULT IT IS TO REMAIN BURIED

Though the reasons for it are good.
Bad habits and repetitive motion,
the pushy, brazen seasons
like someone in a bar coming back
to tell you the same story as last time.
After a while, it was like a megamall:
all the stores selling the same things,
and the muzak, the white noise,
the long traipse through parking lots,
the bags heavy, the money gone.

How easy it was to dig the warm hole
though the clay was hard, and the rocks
in this place so many Sisyphean toils
on an appropriately minor scale.
How welcoming were the creatures
when I lay down, the shy annelids,
secretive things more leggy than an awards show,
and beetles in bronze armour
blind to their own beauty. What stories
quiet things tell with their silent, pinching mouths.

Still, how difficult it is to remain buried,
the wind's whistle through spruce and alder
like a rumour wanting to be passed on,
and birdsong over the racket of tamarack
carrying messages of berries ripening,
the smell of changes burrowing
even through this argillaceous mask.
Something says open your eyes, the particular
colour of sky at this moment wants witness,
though I'd had enough of it when I disappeared.

How lucky it was I parked the car
near enough but hidden; uprooted offerings
snagged in the wipers, blue plastic roses,
and there's a little more rust, but otherwise.
How green the breeze, how desolate the road,
a cracked continuity through copper barrens,
sunset-lit, an eagle lording over it. Around every turn,
another dangerous passion, dusk a thick coating
on the tongue demanding quaffing.

UNSAID

Of course it's a good deal or why would you call me?
But today it rained so heavily

I had that sense of the earth opening a sinkhole
to swallow me. You know that feeling?

And right now I'm looking at a stack of bills
you could use for building material,

chink them with muddy thoughts, so it's highly unlikely
I can afford your offer, this extra insurance, though admittedly—

a cat is making a face at me through the window;
funny, they always want to live in someone else's house,

what's wrong with them? And if your insurance
covered losses I can hardly find words for,

unnamed stray troubles scratching at the door,
you would find me more closely listening

but a green island is drifting away from me,
each day the sea rising.

All week the pallbearer's gloves were in the car
with a rose that rasped

a trail across the dash on sharp turns,
making the sound things make when they fade

until it fell to the floor at my feet.
I sometimes feel helpless in the passenger seat.

And last night the pallbearer's caress
broke through our separateness.

WITH A KEY TO SOME DOOR IN MY HAND

The hotel room is never as imagined.
The door I stand in front of
with some key in my hand
is not where it should be.
The windows should look east
but bathe me in sunset.
Sometimes they have to repeat
terminal & gate to me time & again:
why do I stand stock-still in disbelief?
Get that woman a pill, a glass of water.
Other times love has walked out
of an upstairs window
and broken its neck on the sidewalk
sometime before dawn,
leaving bereft souls with nothing to face
but the day ahead.
And I have gone with magazines & strawberries
& hope in my heart
to support the recovery of a loved one
only to sit vigil through
all the lights and beeps stilling,
strawberries rotting on the nightstand.
And if you open your mouth now,
I don't know what I'll hear,
only make it good.
Some mornings on these early flights
I take the juice, the coffee,
in a stunned trance
or like an acolyte taking communion,
and some days

I arrive at some city,
my clenched fingers aching,
the key to my own front door
still clutched in my hand.

RICHARD GREENE

1961–

ON SHERBOURNE STREET

I am at home in a high-rise
where at night the voice of being human
is a siren blare or a drunk crying fuck
something or other on Sherbourne Street.
Where I live we make our own danger
and the earth is hardly implicated
in our calamities: the man who tumbles
more storeys than he has years,
and the girls on Isabella who are dying
each night in the arms of Corydon.
Security men wear Kevlar vests
and follow a German Shepherd on a chain
through the hallways of my building.
The old sisters next door recall
when this was a desirable address:
the doorman wore a kind of livery then
and helped with parcels.
In St. James Town, the Caribbean gangs
and the Filipinos watch one another,
skirmish, speak of war that may come.
My friend says I am mistaken
in thinking this place affordable.
But I say there is witness amid decay:
the street blossoms
in placards and buttons to save
the hospital from budget cuts,
and the church refurbishes
Mary and Bernadette in their grotto
for worshippers who pass at morning
and touch the stone.

AT THE COLLEGE

Serpentine, the path unwinds its innocence
from building to building in flickering shade
where my students feed lazy raccoons muffins

and glazed doughnuts, as if to domesticate
the last wild things on this suburban campus,
though nothing can make the few deer unafraid

of engines, words, footfalls, the human rumpus,
or subdue the fox's wily nonchalance
and teach him not to kill anything helpless.

Here, among these fierce and sentimental students,
I stand on the edge of a world not my own,
snatching small goods from the large irrelevance

of what we do, making the old sorrows known
to children bearing their first calamities,
teaching solitudes to the newly alone,

explaining writers' exile to refugees
and notions of intrinsic worth to half-fledged
bankers, already driving smart Mercedes.

Yet they live by their hope, curiously pledged
to some afterness that will reward and bless
them for gifts that nature leaves unacknowledged

or earnest labours I grade at B or less;
they know some need of love that poets speak to,
and few can absent their hearts from every class,

however many dronings they may sleep through;
they will mark a perfect image or a phrase
and hear it years from now, wilder then and new.

BESIDE THE FUNERAL HOME

Twice a month, I watch special delivery
of modish coffins for customers anxious
not to be caught dead in the ordinary

or to neglect the last public decencies
and thus send parent, aunt or cousin abroad
again with no mark of comfort or success.

The undertaker's under-men gravely load
each empty coffin onto a folding cart
and then walk it from the alley to be stowed

behind a show-room where any broken heart
costs twelve grand and death looks like a Pontiac,
chrome-detailed and rust-proofed in every part.

But once cigarettes are stubbed on the sidewalk
and a monk in saffron robe has struck the gong
the cortège is led out by the Cadillac.

Cars reach slowly into traffic and are gone,
a sad departure for these new arrivals,
from a funeral home that calls itself "Wing On."

APPARITIONS

It is the Feast of Our Lady of Lourdes;
this parish church, named for her, is crowded
as though it were Easter or Christmas Eve.
Once white as Rosedale, the congregation
is Filipino, Tamil, Caribbean,
their Canada a few acres of shabby
towers across the street, the most densely
populated place on the continent.
Even the white men here are outsiders,
not husbands and fathers, but gay couples
who live in the streets just east of Yonge,
that other estrangement in the city's core.
The back of the bulletin advertises:
"Catholic Cemeteries," a pawn-broker,
"Alleluia Driving School—You're in Safe Hands!"
psychotherapy, two lawyers, a doctor,
and, always, firms providing "Remittances
To Manila," for mothers to send home
the scant harvest of minimum wage
to babes who know them as a photograph
or a voice down the telephone wire.
            I wonder at their fervour, the worshippers
of Mary, their stories of miracles,
healings, locutions, apparitions,
souls released from purgatory by prayers
to her, devotions "never known to fail."
The Tamils leave cookies beside statues,
and at the grotto, candles, money, toys,
in December, a coat for the shoulders of
Bernadette, lest she shiver in the light.

There is only a little extravagance
between this and my grandmother's yearly
pilgrimage to Ste Anne de Beaupré
or my mother's daily Rosary
and roll-call of the dead who, she believes,
will feel the betrayal in her own death
when no one prays for them.
                    My feast is elsewhere
but not separate: my son's seventh birthday,
the third I have missed in as many years.
We celebrated with a phone call,
not long because his party was going on;
it was time to open gifts, and his friends
were there.
              My pang is less in this company,
their accents rippling the surface of hymns
that pour from childhood: "Immaculate Mary,
your praises we sing, you reign now in heaven
with Jesus our King…." The Rosary booms
from speakers wrapped in plastic, the Joyful
Mysteries counted off, as the crowd
circles the church in a slow procession
to pray at the Grotto. Rain falls steadily
and umbrellas blossom under street-lights,
as each of us holds a taper in wet hands.
I see in their faces a flickering grace
and glimpse my son wishing on his day's candles.

1000X

The profusion of the microscope:
I live with my wife and child
among uncatalogued species of pleasure
that swim past like sudden tadpoles.
I can find no scale for the lesser miracles,
a domestic existence
whose landscapes are a table-top,
a bed-sheet and a sink,
whose horizons are paint and plaster,
and whose constellations
are filaments minutely hung.
Love is a conversation in a water-drop.

CUSTOM

The world is drifting further from this world
and every hope is inwardly compelled
from nervousness and acts compounding noise
to strange exclusions and darkening surprise.

I imbibe new silence with every breath
and my range of purpose grows less and less
for clear beyond the customs of this heart
my life is drifting endlessly apart.

WHALER

Great-grandfather,
       whaler out of Nantucket,
the harder sort
       who threw the harpoon,
       drew warm blood,
made huge death on the open sea.

Came home one year
       to find his land fenced
for ecclesiastical uses,
       tore it all down,
told the priest to go to hell,
       and would do his own praying
            after that.

Sailed till his knees went stiff
       with beri-beri
on a ship stuck
       in Antarctic ice.

My father worshipped him,
       remembered his deft hands
that could "put an arsehole in a crackie"
       with a hammer and a handsaw.

       The old man signalled
his affections:
       crafty hard of hearing,
heard the boy's words,
       even took his daughter's orders
           when she called him "Sir!"

Grew old jigging cod
        on the southern shore,
then fell from a roof
        and lingered days to tell
                his last stories,
empty his mouth of good oaths.

What I have of him
        is my father's reverence for
his silence,
        a sense that pain will kill you
if you speak of it.

THE WHITE FLEET

I

Barefoot, they played football beside their ships,
the fishermen of Portugal's White Fleet:
hard tackles on the planking and concrete,
and always foreign tongues shouting pleasure
in tones unmistakable to a boy
who watched old leather fly to makeshift
goals among the nets and ropes and barrows.
The ships, docked three abreast, filled the harbour
with a swaying thicket of masts and yards
and the white blaze of their clustered hulls.
I cannot imagine how it must have seemed
at night on the Banks, their city of lights
over black waters that teemed with cod
but in port they were magical enough
to paint the town with rough benevolence,
a giving of half their lives, year by year,
to the fishing grounds and this Irish place.

II

I am five or six, holding my father's hand,
looking onto the deck of a square-rigger,
one of the last that could have laboured
on the open sea, this fleet's centuries
salted and stacked in a shadowy hold,
a few men on deck, olive faces burned
dark by sealight: they stand for thousands.

III

Two lives, divided by sea and season,
some fathering casually in St. John's
children they might not speak of in Lisbon
when Autumn sailed them to their legal loves.
As for the rest, they were faithful or cheap,
fished abroad and bred quietly at home.
In a city of rum-drinkers, they drank
the wine that traveled with them, sold brandy
on the dock to the bootlegger women.
Public order bore with their offences,
and the constabulary made nothing
of loud drunkenness and small affrays,
because their charities stood in balance:
at any late hour, a Portuguese crew
would genially pour out their twenty pints
to save some stranger bleeding at St. Clare's.

IV

They rowed out, single men in their dories,
as the ship stood to seaward like a wall
built hard against the ocean's killing depth.
They paid out trawls, hooks baited with caplin
or squid, and hauled in the twisting cod
until their boats brimmed with silver thrashing.
Then pulling the oars back and back they brought
the dories to the ship, loaded their catch
in lowered tubs, and climbed out of the sea.
But sudden mists came on the Banks, white ships
vanished, and there was nothing to row for
but the fog-horn sounding on a muffled deck.
Easy enough to pass all safety by,
go in circles or row far past the ship
towards a swamping on the open sea.

V

Fishermen in procession from their ships
carry Our Lady of Fatima
up through the city's winding Old World streets
to the Basilica of the Baptist—
this to honour Mary in their other home
and to make a tighter kinship in her prayers
with those who got the gist of an Ave.
That was years before I was even born.
Their virgin stands now in a shrine beside
the altar, kindly and bland and southern
in the midst of a severe architecture,
out of place among terrible stone saints.
I look for the fishermen in their gift
and find that they are barely knowable:
their hands hardened by rope and oars and salt,
hers a little pale plaster outstretched;
their sailors' eyes narrowed by the sun,
hers widened toward the light's clemency.
And yet she, Stella Maris, was the prayer
they uttered when they left port in blessed ships,
the prayer for plenty, the prayer for passage.
Fish and fishers gone, she prays for them still,
their dangers passed and all petitions moot.

VI

Something ended: thirty years of dragnets
harrowed the seabed to a kind of hell.
I cannot remember when the last white ships
went through the Narrows, old friendships extinct,
and the ocean breeding only grievance.

At the far end of the harbour I watch
a container ship swallowing cargo,
and, before me, three or four fishing boats
roped to the wharf waiting for a good year.
So many lifetimes of the Portuguese
are berthed in the silence of this afternoon,
as their voices ring to a quietness
in memory, just at the moment's edge,
where sunlight reflects on moving water
a bounty beyond our best intentions.

CROSSING THE STRAITS

The sea is moving under our passage,
an old year out and a new year in
between Port aux Basques and North Sydney.
The ship rolls in the first breaths of a gale;
it has been so long, ten or twelve years,
since I last sailed, I do not trust my legs
or stomach to hold against the weather,
so lie still as a narrow berth allows,
reminding myself that disaster
is a kind of lottery, and to sink
as hard as winning millions on dry land,
and that sailors, having made profession
of storms, know their work and die old.
In an hour, anxiety drowns in sleep;
the mind, as ever, opposes passage,
and I dream of my flat in Toronto,
its wooden deck stretching across the roof,
a ship remote from this night's turning.
At six I wake and walk through lounges
where some have sat up all night playing cards
or talking, their New Year's revels queasy
and circumspect where the ship's movement
began the hangovers before the drinks.
More have slept in the rows of La-Z-Boys
before an almost bloodshot T.V. screen,
its hoarse voice still croaking festively
about the crowds that gathered in Times Square.
The gales have subsided and the sea is calm
less than an hour out of North Sydney;
a heavy breakfast later, I walk along
a deck where snow-crusted lifeboats are hung.
I imagine that in summer this is

the ship's best place, but the air is frigid
this morning, and Newfoundlanders crossing
the Straits see water enough in warmer times
to forego the prospect now, but this moment
of pent chances, between home and home,
is not mine alone, and for most who travel
there is some tear in memory between
the longed for and the given, what they left
and what they are. Nova Scotia looms,
and the purser summons drivers to cars
in the ship's belly, where tractor-trailers
are already roaring for landfall.

MICHAEL CRUMMEY
1965–

OLD WIVES' TALES

Except it wasn't a wife talking, or a woman for that matter. It was Charlie Rose at the house to see Father. I was only five or six years old and not even a part of the conversation, sitting under the kitchen table with the dog, listening to the men talk. Charlie said you had to get one before it learned to fly and split its tongue. Right down the middle, he said, and when the crow found the use of its wings it would be able to speak, Arthur, the same as you or I at this table.

You know how a child's mind works. The dog was just a pup then, three or four months old, a yellow Lab. A hot summer that year, we were sitting outside the day after Charlie's visit, her mouth open, panting, the thin tongue hanging there as pink and wet as the flesh of a watermelon. I loved that animal, I just wanted to hear her speak is all. Went in the house and brought out Mother's sewing shears, held one side of the tongue between my thumb and forefinger. The line down the centre like a factory-made perforation meant as a guide for the scissors.

What a mess that dog made when she drank, water slopping in all directions, her tongue split like a radio antennae, the separate leaves flailing as she lap-lap-lapped at the bowl. And not a word in her head for all that.

KITE

I was crooked as a rainbow when I was a boy, I'll admit it. Stabbed Hollis with a pocket knife down on the Labrador. Swung at him with a berry can and split his head open. He'd have beat the snot out of me on more than one occasion if I wasn't the faster runner.

He read something about Marconi's kites one summer and made one for himself out of brown paper and scrap wood; it had a tail ten feet long with bits of coloured rag tied every foot. He worked on it for a week in the old shed, and I chased him out into the meadow garden when he finished it. A perfect day for a kite, a brisk easterly and mostly clear. Helped him get it up and stood beside him as he let out yard after yard of string, the kite pulling taut like an anchored boat in a tide, the narrow wake of the tail snaking behind it. And I'm tugging at Hollis' sleeve, wanting to hold it myself; he's leaning back to keep it high in the wind and telling me no, no way, fuck off, it's my kite, no.

Crooked as a rainbow, like I said. I stomped off toward the house, wishing him dead. When I reached the edge of the garden the kite caught a downdraft, arcing to the ground like a hawk after a rabbit, as if my contrariness had sucked the very wind out of the sky behind me. It landed nose first ten feet in front of where I stood. Hollis was running in my direction, yelling something I couldn't hear over the sound of the wind and I wouldn't have listened anyway. So angry by then I wanted to do something unforgivable. Put both my feet through the kite where it lay and then I ran like hell.

Now he's gone I wish he'd caught up to me that day. Maybe he would have given me something to remember him by, the mark of his hand on my body somewhere. The thin line of a scar I could hold him with a while longer, before the sky carried him off for good.

NEWFOUNDLAND SEALING DISASTER

Sent to the ice after white coats,
rough outfit slung on coiled rope belts,
they stooped to the slaughter: gaffed pups,
slit them free of their spotless pelts.

The storm came on unexpected.
Stripped clean of bearings, the watch struck
for the waiting ship and missed it.
Hovelled in darkness two nights then,

bent blindly to the sleet's raw work,
bodies muffled close for shelter,
stepping in circles like blinkered mules.
The wind jerking like a halter.

Minds turned by the cold, lured by small
comforts their stubborn hearts rehearsed,
men walked off ice floes to the arms
of phantom children, wives; of fires

laid in imaginary hearths.
Some surrendered movement and fell,
moulting warmth flensed from their faces
as the night and bitter wind doled out

their final, pitiful wages.

THE LATE MACBETH

His body divorced him slowly
like a flock of birds leaving
a wire, one set of wings at a time—
still in sight, but past retrieving.

Extremities first, his right foot
dropping asleep, forcing a limp
until the left faltered numb,
conspiring to abort every step.

Fingers and tongue deadened, as if
wrapped in a muffle of feather down—
each affliction painless and shameful,
like a ship run aground in sand.

His infant child seemed to chase him,
her development a mirror
image of his progressive loss;
her wonder, reversed, his terror.

Still, he got on with things, wrote
the last poems, read. Tried to swallow
the panic that galled his throat,
never mentioned the dream of crows.

After his voice abandoned him
his wife scissored an alphabet
and they relearned the grace of words:
letters raised like a wick, and lit.

At the end he was stripped of all
but that fire, its sad, splendid
glow. When his wife offered him
the sedative they knew would end it

he asked "How long will I sleep?"
spelled it out, letter by letter.
The fear had left them both by then.
She told him, "Until you're better."

ARTIFACTS

An old couple lived here before you and I.
Brother and sister, raised in this house,
forced home after years away
by a stingy pension, the death of a spouse.

They didn't get on at all in the end,
the neighbours say, led separate lives,
divided the six rooms between them,
ate separate meals at appointed times.

Stuffed in a drawer, we found sheets of paper
columned with scores, their names scrawled at the top—
they must have argued over words for years
till first the Scrabble, then the talking stopped.

A sad story told by sad artifacts
we never thought might spell out our own.
A house divided as if split by an axe.
Two people sitting to their meals alone.

THE NAKED MAN

Shower room's peace shattered by boys launched
like rockets, their racket sudden as rain
on a tin roof. Shyness sharp as a sprain
makes him wince at the sight of his paunch,

his penis crouched in its thicket of curls.
But the boys ignore the naked man beside
them, their voices pitched toward registers
beyond hearing, skin translucent white,

everything about them in ascendance,
inching toward their adult heights
without hesitation or reluctance.
They orbit his silence like satellites

trailing the dead weight of stars—
there's no way to warn them what lies ahead
and he's torn by a father's helpless regret,
seeing them so unguarded, so free of scars.

THE SELECTED

On a short haul flight to Boston
with *The Selected Paul Durcan*,
Irish lines conjuring the Catholic
girl who taught me to neck—
her mouth a marriage of cigarettes
and Wrigley's spearmint,
my hands two raw cadets
assigned their permanent
station: the blue denim
circling those extravagant hips.

And younger, stalking minnows
in a pond set among spruce
trees beside the Catholic manse;
the handsome Father who
played tennis in white shoes,
who flew his own plane,
and eventually renounced
the priesthood for a woman.

All the way to Logan
International, the twinge
of something left behind
at the airport in Halifax
while waiting for my connection,
a loss I can't coax
clear of faint apprehension.
The stewardess leans in
to offer a tray of snacks,
a small silver crucifix
tick-tocking below her perfect
smile, one immaculate hand
marred by the fleck
of a gold wedding band.

BOYS

Not old enough to pay for our trouble,
or even name it, we wandered the town

after dark like dogs, half-tamed at best.
We set small fires and hurled rocks and pissed

against school doors, nosing the margin
of the disallowed, the out of bounds.

We ranged as far as the train trestle,
sniffing underbrush and the long grass

for anything dead or lost or unusual,
broke into empty buildings for the thrill

of stealing through forbidden spaces,
of standing at darkened windows, invisible

while the innocent traffic drove past.
We perched at the lip of change, we knew it,

though in our eyes time itself stood still,
we couldn't imagine ourselves at thirty

or married or living other places—
what we wanted was to see the world undress,

to lie down naked somewhere dirty
and fuck, to do all the unspeakable

things our green minds could only intuit,
a communal urge we suffered alone.

Half-grown, we were living our life by halves,
our dreams were vacant rooms we didn't own

and roamed in silence, shadows behind dark glass,
our mute hearts a mystery to ourselves.

GIRLS

Their bodies were stripling and sleek
and more or less like our own

but for the one alien nook
that made them partial to skirts

and the Easy-bake oven,
clumsy with a hockey stick—

it was the only explanation
the world offered for their eccentric

habits, their feminine quirks,
and it was too simple and stark

a truth to be refuted:
you stood or sat to take a piss

which was the final word on
how a soul was constituted.

Even the beauties who were rough
and tumble, who were known to pick

a fight and could use their fists
carried that internal question mark,

a riddle we couldn't solve or evade.
They were a fruitless provocation,

a rattling kernel of magic
we pretended did not exist,

ten years old and already afraid
we'd never get far enough

inside that cleft's niggling divide
to understand what makes them tick.

FOX ON THE FUNK ISLANDS

She drifted down from the Strait on an ice pan
and played havoc with the breeding season,

the only predator within fifty miles—
wandering the well-stocked aisles,

chasing seabirds off their roosts for the tasty
morsel of fresh eggs, gorging on the delicacy,

and she killed a freezer-load of adults as well,
caching the carcasses she was too full

to eat, an ancient northern instinct, a store
against the meagre months of winter.

We gave her no chance on the Funks
after the colony migrated, thinking once

snow settled in on that deserted ground
she would starve to death or drown

in the bottomless cold, too rich
an appetite for an economy so strict,

but she was waiting for us in June
having survived the winter dark alone,

making a long celebratory meal
of anything she could chase down and kill.

The returning birds unsettled, too skittish
to lay or tend their chicks in the nest,

and all summer we set traps, hoping to take
her alive; each time she stole the bait,

leaving some small gift in trade,
a razorbill's head, a puffin's wing laid

beside the trigger inside the useless device
as a thank you or a taunt, and once or twice

a week she hung near the camp to watch us,
her stare calm and intently curious.

We were an inconsequential riddle
on the margins of her concern, an idle

interest indulged at her leisure,
and what she made of us being there

preoccupied our talk as we picked away
at the summer's banding survey,

imagining ourselves in her predicament,
anomalous and intransigent,

wild and sovereign, hopelessly astray—
and we admired the creature, grudgingly.

Shot her our last week out there before the boat
arrived, and we each laid a hand to the ratty coat

as if to apologize for the necessary offence,
a gesture of awkward, amoral reverence.

DATSUN

Dumped and torched in the White Hills decades back
and everything remotely organic—
cushions, tires and vinyl, interior fabric—
long ago stripped from the scrawny wreck
by fire, by decay's reckoning *tick tick tick*.
All year it squats there, listing off the track
in the approximate shape of a ransacked
four-door sedan with automatic
transmission, though each season the trick
is less convincing and that rusting lock,
soon enough, will be impossible to pick.

Meantime, the woods improvise a meadow
in its coldframe, seeding the import's hollow
shell with alder, with fern and willow,
all craning their heads out a window
or doors hanging ajar, a wayward crew
on a summer road trip, the Datsun's slow
collapse just countryside they're passing through.

KEEL

There was nowhere the soil gave
enough to spade a proper grave—
placed the man in a shallow cleft
above the landwash, clasped hands,
dead eyes coppered to a close.
His own boat tipped face down
where he lay, marker and coffin,
rough seal chinked tight with moss,
the gunwale skirted with stones
before we left the little craft
on the darkest deepest ocean
with its solitary passenger—
upturned keel carving a slender
channel through the seasons,
drifting each cloudless night across
crowded shoals of constellations.

AGNES WALSH

1950–

THE TIME THAT PASSES

The time that passes between my mother and me
is more measured in what's not said,
and plain words are felt like samplings of fabrics.

Body, she said, we never said body then,
it was too bold, we said system:
tell the doctor what part of your system hurts.

I linger,
hold onto the feel,
the rub in the mind.

If they left it alone, Mike said,
and someone got hurt, then they'd be blempt for it.

I hold onto before, before our
tongues were twisted around corrected speech.

He was so grand he couldn't say Okay,
like the rest of us,
he said *Oh Kah*.

I ranted that we're educated into ignorance,
but can get jobs on the mainland
or at radio stations,
our voices do sound so homogeneous now.

> But you watch it, my mother said,
> it's your tongue too that was dipped
> in the blue ink, and do go leaking iambics
> all the day long.

OUR BOARDER ALFRED,
HE MUST HAVE BEEN 300 POUNDS

Our kitchen table sits three comfortably. When Alfred arrived with his heavy brown suitcase, our kitchen bulged and moaned and seemed to try and move over to make room. Our table dropped its lower lip and sighed. We were expecting grave discomforts and had second thoughts.

Alfred worked days and returned at 4:45. He rolled his sleeves up to his elbows, and carefully washed his face and forearms. After, as he buttoned his cuffs, he hummed and smiled at his good fortune—whatever it was. Then he turned and entered our kitchen like a whale in a rain puddle. We talked about this when Alfred wasn't around, and decided it wasn't because he was so big, but because we were so short, and women, and the kitchen was so small. We just weren't used to him, so silent, and a man. His voice was tiny, we had to keep saying: "Pardon me, Alfred. What was that?" And he'd smile at the most tedious questions, like a tired lion who loved little mice.

One day our backdoor blew off and Alfred went to his brown suitcase and got a hammer and nails—although we had our own. When he had fixed it, he took, to our double surprise, a dented four-stop accordion out of the same suitcase. He lifted up a kitchen chair with one hand, and with his accordion in the other, he went out onto the back doorstep. The instrument wheezed and squealed. Alfred went into a trance. We stood in the porch and looked at each other and at Alfred's big arms moving in and out. When he finished he looked up and grinned. "I'm rusty," he said, "and that's the first in ages I've played for the public."

When the Trade School was built, Alfred gave us his notice. He smiled and said: "I've to leave you soon ladies for my next job." We didn't know how to take that and had to pinch ourselves. We tried to be more generous with the jam, made wider pancakes, put less milk in the mashed potatoes. But Alfred zipped up his brown suitcase one evening and patted it on the side. Out of his windbreaker pocket he produced a bottle of Captain Morgan and smiled as he put it on the table. We got down glasses and boiled water. Then Alfred talked. The walls expanded, puffed out, and then breathed in when he raised his glass to his lips. We were glad that, no matter how far the rum went down in the bottle, he never talked dirty. We were nervous because we never drank much and always went to Mass on Sunday.

We said: "Alfred, stay the night because the roads are bad." But he smiled, floated his glass onto the table, got up and shook our hands. We watched through the front window as he opened the taxi door. The snow tried to bury his bulk. It's no night for travelling we thought, and waved through the glass.

Inside our kitchen, we cleaned up and sat down to look at each other. The walls moved in, the ceiling settled its shoulders upon our heads. The table shrank to a miniature night stand. Why didn't everything expand? We wondered what to do with all the space that we could hold in our cupped hands.

When we went to the door to lock up, Alfred was still struggling to get into the car.

PERCY JANES BOARDING THE BUS

I was going to the Mall for a kettle
waiting on the number five,
when the number something-or-other
pulled up.

I was looking past it for mine,
when I saw him, an arm raised,
running softly.

I jumped to life, beat on the bus door,
said to the driver: "Mr. Janes.
Mr. Percy Janes wants to get on."

He raised a "So what?" eyebrow.

Mr. Janes straightened his astrakhan hat,
mumbled thank you and stepped up.
As the bus rumbled on
I continued under my breath:
"Ladies and gentlemen, Mr. Percy Janes,
Newfoundland writer, poet,
just boarded the number something-or-other."

If this was Portugal,
a plaque would be placed
over the seat where he sat.

As it is, you have me
mumbling in the street
like a tourist in my own country.

I SOLEMN

My mother scrubbed my face and braided my hair.
She told me to put on my dark blue corduroy dress,
the good thick one from Aunt Mary. She laid the crescent
of hat on her head and stuck a long white pin
with a pearled end into it. (And her head?) It
went in so deep but she didn't jump or cry out, or even wince.
What she did was pull the veil down from its fold until
it rested against her nose.

And gloves. Hers black and mine white.
"You must be very serious. And don't be scared, there's
nothing to be scared about. It's only death, and death can't
hurt you." She took me by the hand and closed the door
behind us and turned the key.

It was my first time for death. I was thought big enough.
So we walked down Swan's road to Mrs. Corrigan's.
The sun was all hallelujah and gave the grass that warm,
green smell. My friends were swinging in the playground,
singing "itsy bitsy teenee weenee yellow polka-dot bikini
that she wore for the first time today." "Look straight ahead,"
my mother said, "be solemn." And I was, although my shoes
pinched. I looked at the clouds moving
fast in the sky above and felt that shiver of life
when it holds you and shakes you between not knowing
and knowing *something*.

Men were outside the door smoking cigarettes
with tams pushed back, dressed up like Sunday.
One man moved himself off the door frame and said "Alice."
Mom said "Francis." Inside was like going into dark night.
The room was full of women and two nuns. Along the back

wall a long, black, shiny box, sleek as a trout. There were
rosary beads on laps and faces flattened with sorrow.

Up! I was swooped up and held above the box and
inside was the meringue of a lemon pie and a woman
lying in the meringue. Not really Mrs. Corrigan who used to
yell and chase us with the broom and tell us we should be
tied to the clothesline. She was far away, tired and cold.
"Kiss her on the hands," my mother whispered. My lips
felt pink, her hands felt white.

On the floor again I was given a triangle of ham sandwich
and a saucer of hot, sweet tea. "She's a grand good girl now
after going to a poor soul's wake." And all the women smiled
sorrowfully at me. And I solemn.

Solemn as could be.

THE LAYING OUT, 1956

Wash the corpse, put on the habit,
put the pennies on the eyelids,
the prayer book under the jaw,
fold the arms with the rosary beads
entwined around the fingers,
stop the clock, turn the looking glass
to the wall, knock him on the forehead
with the hammer to make sure he's dead.

STORM

Heavy rain blowing in sheets woke me.
At the window I looked to sea, out past
the harbour wondering if there were boats out,
remembering my father's death and life.

I had walked into the hospital ward
as he was coming up from under the anaesthetic.
His arms stretched over his head tracing
swift, definite movements in the air.

A voice behind me said: "Don't worry, love.
He's mending sails, and then he's tacking home."
I sat down by his bed, tranced as he was,
my eyes following the fragile web of his fingers.

Later when he was himself, he whispered:
"Do you know who that is in the bed across the way?
That's Captain Jim Harris. Go speak the Portuguese to him."

We talked of Aveiro, Oporto, Lisboa,
of the sun, and the wine, and the *fado*.
I felt my father's pride at me speaking Portuguese
to the best sailing captain out of Placentia Bay.

My father so tiny in the bed. Time stealing him from me.
I sat and listened to him and the captain
talk of weather, fish and old schooners—
what he had talked of all his life.

He'd call tonight a bad one.
Hurricane Louis would drive him from his bed,
send him down the hall in his stocking vamps
checking the stove, the doors and windows,
making us warm and watertight.

And tonight
I feel like howling into the fury
to bring him back safe to me.

KEN BABSTOCK
1970–

CAMPING AT GLENDALOUGH

A goat-track, for hours, a gorse-edged trough
that fanned to a dusted bristle of heather.
We pitched our pegless tent on the crest
where it lifted, exhaled, a lung
on a ledge, ballooning in the wind's
high whip—we set the corners
with pocked stone, laughed at the thought
of it flung over the edge, blown
like a spore at the two lakes below. We hollowed
out a bowl between scrub pine and
must have struck then tossed every match
in a box before the meshed stook
of dried twigs caught, licked
out, looked over at the opposite face
where sheep like snow-patches slipped
and levelled from crevice to crack.
I heard the moan of fallen arches and
began bad-mouthing the long trek back. Perhaps
we'll stay, push on, higher, west where
the haze of cirrus fades to a passport
black, star-stamped and shut, not just
expat but exhuman; gone hairy, sure footed,
at home with our funk, reading the cairns
of warm dung like prayers before lunch.
I wanted to say something then, just mouth
the option but an old law hung like a beard
in my head. Still unsure: theoretical physics
or high-flown Yeats verse, the thrust
of it was how conditions may
shift from bad toward worse.

FINISHING

Every mitre only as clean as the chop saw
it's cut on. Any gouge, puncture, or flaw

in baseboard or casing is quickly forgiven
by almighty Spackle; your putty knife turns uneven

joints into smoothline, turns nickel-sized hammer dents
back into the wood's true profile—

                        at the owner's expense.

Thin wainscotting strips are worthless poker hands
you keep throwing back to watch land

at attention, soldier-straight, from the bathroom door
right down the corridor's

parade route. That easy. That fast. And if the framing's well built—
no vicious lean, tilt,

or bad wow—the aesthetics should be clear, even simple,
like topping a self-portrait in oils with an eye-pleasing dimple

that doesn't exist in real life.
How else to render a bland, formless grief

into something at least sellable? The mere appearance of beauty's
not beauty, but it's reliable.

Just finish. Get paid.
At night, alone, you'll redeem or undo what your hands have made.

CARRYING SOMEONE ELSE'S INFANT PAST A COW IN A FIELD NEAR MARMORA, ONT.

Summer gnats colonized her molasses black eyes, her flicking,
conical ears. She moaned, a badly tuned
tuba, and tassels of ick dripped
from her black-

on-pink nostrils like strings of weed sap. Waking from a rhythmic
nap in my arm, you wobbled your head upright
and stared at the great hanging skin-
bag, teats, dry-docked

hull of her ribs, anvil head, and the chocolate calm in her eyes
that gazed back as I carried you closer, wading
through goldenrod, mulleins, thistle
all artfully bent

clear of your soft exposed feet. Ants worried the punky
tops of knotted fence posts, and caution flags
of gossamer and milkweed fluff
marked each rust-twist

of barb, but that was all that divided you and her. I felt briefly
happy to be prop, peripheral in this exchange,
this unfolding bundle of knowing that
was you in

an overgrown ditch where the air swelled, shaking itself dry
in the sumac. What was I shown that I haven't retained?
What peered back long before the cracked
bell of its name

came sounding off a tongue's hammer and fenced it forever? Know
that it happened, though—you were a drooling lump
of living in the verdant riddle. That heifer
remembers

nothing of you. Let chicory, later in life, be bothersome blue
asterisks footnoting one empty, unrecoverable
hour of your early and
strange.

THE 7-ELEVEN FORMERLY KNOWN AS RX

Back in the day, I was proud of my vast palette
of candies; those for a penny over the front
counter, for kids and grannies, and the more
potent display locked in the back cabinet,

only ever given away if you'd come with a note
declaring you blocked, arthritic, headachy
or just couldn't say what was wrong for the frog
in your throat. Now, I sell mouthfuls of salt

to the stoned. It was snug in here, I was kept
stocked and swept by a family of five from Lisbon.
Now I'm grudgingly manned by tattooed kids
in green tunics helping themselves to the porn. And

the light in me's a perpetual migraine, I'm a super-
nova on a quiet corner, beacon to that fleet
of 4Runners and Acuras disgorging their thunder
of hip hop and jungle. I haven't slept since 1983.

To make space for the flavoured coffee station and
an ATM, they knocked out my east wall, expanded
onto the ribbon of lawn—not at all what that Aussie
meant when he defined "sprawl." I used to dream

in flamenco played on a push-button tape deck, or
the gurgle of talk radio on a Saturday, but I'm
lobotomized now, a drooler, listening to the Freon
drone from the dairy and drinks cooler. Gone

the licorice whips, manila envelopes, shampoo,
shaving kits; I'm all Scratch'n Win, *Vanity Fair*,
shellacked fruit, and the crinkling bladders of months-old
chips. I squat in my numbness and stare, recording

each night's parade of freaks on hidden surveillance
film. I'm hyperaware. I've begun to loathe
the intervals between guns when I have to convince
myself I'm still here. Oh, Maria, shelving hockey

cards while muttering lines by Pessoa; Papa's spirals
of suds greasing the glassfront; the boy out back
whacking tennis balls off my brick hip as the day
falls away. We stayed in the black but that

wasn't enough, nor was attaching Rx to the family name.
Atlanta home office faxes directives re: New Promo,
end aisle-ing my insides. They demand perfect rhyme: "I"
ground down, cauterized, shelved in the back of "franchise."

TRACTOR

Like mill wheels through a dark current, its herringbone
treads paddled through clumped earth and stone,

tossing pressed clots of brown dirt off their
upswing to fall, then, and remingle, aerated.

The small hinged cap atop a burping exhaust pipe
flapped in slow panic like the mother killdeer who'd taken a clip

from the tiller blade's edge for playing the martyr:
watched her furrowed nest of three eggs ploughed under

yet kept up her act while the flared cobra hoods
of the hammered rear-fenders cast shadows over sunned clods.

The valentine of the bucket seat perched on spring-coil: a metal palm-
leaf saddle burnished to a beach stone's gleam

that said a scooped-out I love you to any-sized ass.
A grumbling muscle, the grey bowels would hiss

and steam tendrils of mist if a sun shower passed over,
otherwise content, compressed in a throaty, subsurface worksong or

hymn that rattled its tin and heated the field's own dizzying heat.
I seemed to live on the thing when not in the bunkhouse, flat out,

dreaming spindly, front-axle dreams of the earth's intractable
turning under bloated, gear-cog tires that stood still

as they spun. We learned to be emptied, to become pure
function that summer. Dragged, reversing into row after row, acre

upon acre, until distance accordioned, time folded,
moments, hours became interchangeable dead

space our labour languished inside of. Drawing
figure eights with the gleaming hoes we hunched over, avoiding

green seedlings that appeared every other second or so
like metronomic ticks pacing our breathing, becoming a flow

we sat and worked in and ignored, spitting. Our necks gathered sun,
tightened, itched. Not four people pulled on the implement but one,

one, one, and one. Cowed into silence by the Go-Down-Moses,
near-nirvana breadth and bent grind of each day. An aching gnosis

punctuated by deerfly bites or an arm's numbed buzz when
a hoe rang the deep bell of a dislodgeable stone. We had fun,

alone together, dredging up privately what it was like to be elsewhere:
a moored midlake raft, drugged in a rec room, or almost untenable
under

upright acres of mirrored glass, in a seed row of streetlight.

PRAGMATIST

I was on a tractor in the rain
                when it occurred to me, my paternal
                        grandfather was called 'Henry James'

                        and cooked meals for men in a coastal
                lumber camp in Bonavista Bay.
The brother of that other James

was William who wrote on matters spiritual
                and hung with John Dewey. Henry
                        James Babstock's brother's name was Samuel.

                        So this grandfather, who went by 'Pappy,'
                died when I was two. He
was a huge man, gentle, happy,

and given to tossing infants in the air.
                Concerning one's self only
                        with the task at hand while temporarily

                        ignoring metaphysics has had more
                recent support from the American
thinker Richard Rorty. His name

sounds like a tractor coughing, revving,
                having sat idle in a field in the rain.
                        When I was two, and at the zenith

                        of one of Henry James's loving pitches—
                up near the ceiling of a white clapboard
house that has since been taken down, or

outdoors above the porch, or 'bridge'
          as he and his wife Alma
                    would have called it—I was at the edge

                    of something. That descent, and all my
          subsequent nothings and entanglements,
loves, riots, slippages, and cries,

could be felt to have happened inside a quiet
          afterthought; a kind of dimming down
                    of who I was when I was him and contained.

                    Turn now to a book by William James
          on states of religious experience.
I was pulling a trailer onto which

a friend was loading irrigation pipes.
          He was powerful, and beautiful, yet
                    far from me, we finished early to a round

                    of applause from a bank of thundercloud
          that had reared up over the cottonwoods.
There's a kind of shroud I pull across my life.

THE MINDS OF THE HIGHER ANIMALS

are without exception irresponsible. Which
sounds alarming and is, admittedly, an aberration
(perhaps not funny) of a more valid, thinkable notion,
that dolphins, wolves, chimps, etc., flip a switch

in us, casting klieg light on the frightening solitude
engendered by the very Fifties idea—I know—
that we alone are responsible for our own
consciousness. A friend, who'd taken work as tutor

to a high-school student, leaned over the back wall
of a booth in a pub and told me: of all the thumbnail
sketches he'd done for her, from *Plato* to *Pascal*
and beyond, this Sartrean concept of taking ownership over all

that you know, feel, and do, had proved the most opaque,
the singularly *most inconceivable stupidity*
ever designed to befall a girl, driving her to kick some shitty
desk chair in frustrated disbelief. Now, Reader, make

a face that's meant to express some woeful sense
of pity and surprise, while feeling a cold sickness underneath.
That was my face. I was mumbling things so far from the truth
of what I felt, I could have been a clergy entering the manse,

touching tops of heads, asking how days went, seeking food,
while wishing one or the other end of this circus dead.
The sight of a pint glass didn't cause me to vomit. I didn't
reel, sweating and murderous, out into the street; but my mood

stiffened, grew intractable, opaque; I felt blue flashes inside
that were flares of all the moments I'd sought causality,
a why for each failing of character, somewhere outside
of myself, amounting to a web of reflexive sophistry

that reached back into the years of my life like illness
discovered late, or how rot sets into wood compromising
the strength of a structure by softening its centre. Rising
from my seat, I went and faced a woman whose caress

had eased my passage through some months I couldn't pass
through on my own, she'd been more than kind, I'd
found I couldn't love her at the time, and fled.
So I faced her, and apologized as best I could, given the mass

of people in the pub. 'This is a poem,' she said, 'and that's not
good enough. Around here, we don't let art, no matter
how acutely felt, stand in for what's necessary, true, and right.
Next time you face me, maybe leave you here. End quote.'

MATERIALIST

Where I put my palm to the crushed
        granite exterior, to the tooled wood
            of the portico's columns

            banded by afternoon sun, I
        thought I could feel where rain
had earlier that day slickened, cooled

then warming, vanished. There'd been
        an interlude of rain. The sun made
            a cracking sound and resumed breathing.

            Our coats opened. The hemmed
        end of yours clawed a jar of preserves
from its place on a deli shelf. Red Sicily

expanding in a laminate sea. Where Prince
        Arthur leaves the Main, sets and subsets
            of visitors, kids, residents drew Venn

            diagrams around buskers. I went
        toward the gaunt, tinny sound of spoons,
fiddles, expecting farce or illness. About being

loved, and returning love, we'll say it heats
        the surface in its passing, then becomes
            surface, a tactile skin on the world

              our eyes feel in photons, chiasmic
        inversion of what's purportedly there. You
at the edge of the gathering watches

you at the gathering's edge. So it
              would seem. Montreal; 3 p.m. in the strange
                    warmth, aren't we now hung on the rack

              of the problem of some smaller 'you'
        happier left—or kept—alone? Tiny mote,
mote's opposite, unmeasured, entirely featureless

but for its property of denied emergence. The music
        fell out of a cheap tape deck. Above that
              a plaid-shirted marionette clogged away

              in his scaled-down cabin. Fire flickered
        from a wood stove made of two
thimbles. A rocker set in motion by the footfalls.

Art hung on the walls, and a view onto
        green-blue woods where jays battled
              the hours away; fire-ditch; spring-melt—

              I was warming to the show, when
        the puppeteer removed his hands, stepped out
and clapped along. Then he left, and it went on.

COMPATIBILIST

Awareness was intermittent. It sputtered.
              And some of the time you were seen
                        asleep. So trying to appear whole

                        you asked of the morning: Is he free
              who is not free from pain? It started to rain
a particulate alloy of flecked grey; the dogs

wanted out into their atlas of smells; to pee
              where before they had peed, and might
                        well pee again—though it isn't

                        a certainty. What is? In the set,
              called Phi, of all possible physical worlds
resembling this one, in which, at time *t*,

was written 'Is he free who is not free—'
              and comes the cramp. Do you want
                        to be singular, onstage, praised,

                        or blamed? I watched a field of sun-
              flowers dial their ruddy faces toward
what they needed and was good. At noon

they were chalices upturned, gilt-edged,
              and I lived in that same light but felt
                        alone. I chose to phone my brother,

over whom I worried, and say so.
He whispered, lacked affect. He'd lost
my record collection to looming debt. I

forgave him—through weak connections,
through buzz and oceanic crackle—
immediately, without choosing to,

because it was him I hadn't lost; and
later cried myself to sleep. In that village
near Dijon, called Valley of Peace,

a pond reflected its dragonflies
over a black surface at night, and
the nuclear reactor's far-off halo

of green light changed the night sky
to the west. A pony brayed, stamping
a hoof on inlaid stone. The river's reeds

lovely, but unswimmable. World death
on the event horizon; vigils with candles
in cups. I've mostly replaced my records,

and acted in ways I can't account for.
Cannot account for what you're about
to do. We should be held and forgiven.

AS MARGINALIA IN JOHN CLARE'S
THE RURAL MUSE

I wasn't finished. From as far back
as I can recall having heard a voice in my skull

I've wanted to die, or change, or die
changing. Hexagonal window, the moon

penned in it, and a segmented swarm sucking
up peonies. Heat off tar shingles

in June as the blood in one arm
blackened, thickened, went blearily toxic,

I exited earth up an IV tube.
The wall-mounted paper dispenser

narrating nightmares of scale, sores fell
from fingers—get well petals—and grew

back puce. Slug of little light, the bedrail
gleamed. Warmed yoghurt, a summons

button and visual aphasia. Now I've no spit,
no hospice and admit nothing, or,

for long stretches, only what happened
was all that ever could have happened.

Reeds curtain where land abuts lake,
if such limit exists, if ducks aren't taken

by pike mid-thought.

METHODIST HATCHET

It was too much of a good thing
but at least it's over now. They are making a pageant out of it,
one of them told me.

          —John Ashbery

      I read it somewhere—the derisive
tag the antecedents half-earned scowling at naked wallboards
when yet they clustered

      on their dehiscent jut of oily granite.
In the demographic lacunae between Catholic settlers of Salvage
and Sandy Cove's low Anglicans,

      we *glory-fits*, *swaddlers*, we *Wesleyans*
counted as hypocrites, Janus-faced, joyless, pulpit-pounding cult
members with hypertension. Split

      wood with one, you're alternately
cleaving air. Axe acting the middler to a Christmas spruce is the axe
shaving off a switch

      then notching belt leather. Blade
above the goose's neck bisects the flecked, lashless, hazel sun
like a corneal scratch.

      Tired weight—hear it?—like wet
gabardine, of barking on about moon-dogs' relation to the flight
path of a shrike, rhetoric's

      murres, punishable life, the eddying
surface where potheads submerged. Those unaffected bent to,
tarring up blowy joins,

      greasing refitted outboards, picking
stone from stone, or replaced in the mended day timber slips
time could eat. Holiday

        cabins in rows now, someone's Christ
on cheap veneer, cod stink gone, Nescafé tin, cellophane bay
heaves, settles, but won't

        uncrinkle as crab husks wash up
from the converted fish plant, crowns, their gulls attendant—
Biography's digital file,

        adjusted, piles them totemic, ceramic,
serrated shins, and snaps No; meaning what could I know of it? Place,
position, effect, raised

        a hic in tepid UC milk and water
I talk still like I'm from nowhere, or Ontario, and flood my head
with pretension having

        lapsed since, if that's sayable, like
falling off porch steps into a hedge. Secular self grown peninsulaic,
won't budge, tides and

        unlike elements squeezed in on three
sides but a view of the distant horizon held steady for decades;
cardiograph, whetstone, fine

        thread to lean toward while attached,
mollusc, to a cold central mass. Consider both, do neither. Door key
fob is driftwood. Unleavened

        pillow. Getaway rental ticks over
on lawn as near the storm door as held counsel is to the vatic register.
Word is belief. Check out's eleven.

SUE SINCLAIR
1972–

COLLAR BONES

Why do they make us think
of birds, the spreading of wings?

Only the mind is more in love
with flight. Desire

rises, hinges at the throat:
here is where we glimpse

one another, in the aerodynamics
of bones that skim the neckline, glide

from shoulder to shoulder, two halves
of a single bone healed

separately. Through us
they wish for a lost

amplitude, hint at a symmetry
that might have been.

RED PEPPER

Forming in globular
convolutions, as though growth
were a disease, a patient
evolution toward even greater
deformity. It emerges
from under the leaves thick
and warped as melted plastic,
its whole body apologetic:
the sun is hot.

Put your hand on it. The size
of your heart. Which may look
like this, abashed perhaps,
growing in ways you never
predicted.

It is almost painful
to touch, but you can't help
yourself. It's so familiar.
The dents. The twisted symmetry.
You can see how hard it has tried.

PADDLING

The shine, the square of light on every leaf,
lilies, more leaves, the V of the canoe in the water: gateway
to nowhere, the beginning of imagining you aren't.

Fear of profusion: where things are few, they seem
necessary. The trees and their thousand leaves massed
on the verge of disappearance.

Light clamps onto us, we'll have to skin ourselves
to be rid of it. Paddles dip in the water, dip and pretend
they don't know what goes on, don't see the world vanishing.

In the mind's mud, nothingness spawns. Where time becomes less
pressing, we feel its depth. The world is burnished: trees, bark, skin
going up in flame. The gods are not what you hoped they would be.

The sun, taking us all down with it.
Heedless, the ten thousand things.

FOREVER

Too young to be convinced, you can't imagine
that time might turn itself inside out, showing
that what you thought was the infinite
was only its lining. Slippery and easily frayed,
your whole life a kind of magic trick.

You rehearse your own funeral, who will attend,
who will be sorry, how death will somehow prove you right.
Submerged in thoughts of this death like a bath,
right up to the neck, still breathing.

What you don't want to imagine is how far it will take you
from the known: your friends and relatives will watch your life
close into a fist, from which, when you take your last breath,
they will pull a square of bright silk. They'll slide it through their fingers
then let it go, watch it drift away. And when they're ready,
they'll open the fist to show it's empty.

LILACS

For those who have lived
where lilacs bloom, who have lost
their immunity
                to idleness and wander through
doorway after doorway
when the lilac trees open their infinite
mauve rooms. For those
who give in and glide a little behind
their lives, a hand trailing
in the water
behind a rowboat.

Regret turns itself inside out,
like a glove
you've picked up after someone's
gone. Even the bees feel it,
sadly, sadly,
nose in the flowers,

a curtain pulled away
and there's no hand on your shoulder
to catch you before you lean too far
out the window.

A slow leak, something escaping
as soon as the petals open.
What's left grows twice
as heavy, pales,
sinks inside itself and stays
with you, a dream of which
there is not even enough left
to describe:

it is about to rain.
It is always about to rain.
These limp flowers.

BEFORE YOU WERE BORN

They have taken a step away
from the familiar. Their lives so far
peel like paint, behind it their real existence.
Your father, at the bar,
buys your mother a drink. You are hidden,
painted into the picture but camouflaged.
No one has seen you yet.

They watch the bartender
pull the tap. It shines
like the places they hope to visit,
the plans they don't have yet.

She is a room in a house that lets the light
in slowly. His inner life rests on his face
like a lamp
he's forgotten to turn off.

The visible makes love
to the invisible. People gather
around tables, quivering,
wanting to be taken from darkness
into the flame.

The bartender keeps his wings folded
at his back. Watches. A bottle opener
hangs from a chain on his belt.
The dust on his wings glitters,
rubs off if he's not careful.

The lights are dim, but the mirrors
multiply their faces, send them down
a long corridor. They emerge, repeated,
confirmed. Your mother, your father. Yourself.

Here it is, the secret
they didn't dare believe.
They don't yet know how it will show them home.
They feel their way in the dark.

ORPHEUS MEETS EURYDICE IN THE UNDERWORLD

Still limping, she has come. She waits at the foot of the hill, doesn't dare go further, remembers how it once vanished under her feet.

She has spent the time thinking about her wedding day, tracing the mark on her ankle where the serpent bit. It hasn't healed yet; perhaps it won't until he comes back. She has never desired his death, but wished for it as one wishes for rain.

The steep hill, where it led and couldn't lead. So many times.

When he arrives he looks more tired than she can understand. The lyre has vanished; they stand together silently.

Even as she remembers his face, she loses something else. She has been alone so long now; how often she has stood here, how much she has wanted to climb.

She takes him home, puts him to bed, then slips in beside him. His childhood bed, too short for him now; they will have to find another.

They waken slowly. As ghosts they pass through each other's bodies, she puts her hand into his heart. He has been worried she would forget.

They play in the fields, run races, drift through tall grasses carelessly, as only those who have had to wait forever can. They have a private sign language; no one speaks in this place, even the streams are still.

Sometimes when they are walking she teases him, falls behind. He looks over his shoulder again and again: there she is. They never tire of this game.

SURRENDER

Sometimes the light, a horse,
gallops into the room
and demands you surrender.
It paws the floor, snorts—
and so you rise out of the low-lying
cloud of the self, the half-dreaming
wakefulness we call love,
and into the cool air of the real.

It shakes its mane impatiently,
rears and kicks, its beautiful body
insisting on what it wants,
pushing its way in. Not
that you're afraid, not exactly.
But it shines straight into your eyes.
And though the heart is small
and cramped, barely large enough for
your own wants, you retreat into a corner,
make do with less. Your only choice
when the world lifts its head
and clarity pours from its back.
Filling the room.

BREAKER

A cold-burning brilliance,
distillery of light, green camouflaged
in the ocean's understorey. Your mind is gathered
like a horse about to take a hurdle, ready to leap.
But fascinated by the rising wall, it stalls,
and time seems to slow
while you consider the monumental
fatigue of this immanent failure.

Beauty like a stain bleeds through
the layers of matter,
                    something, somewhere in pain,
the traces of it seeping into this world.
You stand back and watch as the inevitable
takes over: the green recess
of the wave collapses, the light buckles,
the depths recover what was owed.
How helpless you are yet
on the brink of being able to do more,
as though you could punch your hand through
the window to rescue whatever it is that,
trapped inside, haunts the corridors.
You haven't, though, quite got what it takes.
The window shatters anyway, but in the spirit
of denial. So it goes, the heartbreak
of merely standing by as what
dwells here does its living and dying
on its own terms.

BREAKWATER

The boulders lifted from the shore,
raised in slings as though being rescued.
Embarrassed, their awkward bodies
dangle in mid-air as though they had been
woken from sleep, taken unprepared.
Piled like rubble in the bay,
they stare out from the breakwater
as if forbidden to speak, using ancient
telepathy to send a warning.

We were afraid of something they
represented, their blank faces
looking somberly into the future,
monuments to a mistake we had yet
to make, traces of something
we wanted to erase before it could exist.
We haven't eluded it. No better off,
we've forfeited consolation, won't know
where to go in our grief.

We've cast ourselves deliberately out
of our own future; it is a locked door
on which we will bang and bang,
looking for answers, looking for silence,
a moment to think through our lives
before they're lost.

PORTUGAL COVE, NIGHT

The dock lights glow, involuntary,
instinctive. Beyond them, something takes
the form of darkness and enters the world,
a prowling animal laying claim to his territory.
A fire kindles in the gut, a warning—
you're standing so close to this creature
and his infinitude of names.

Shivering, you realize he's the one
you've called on to keep chaos at bay—
how foolish you were. You feel his breath
on your neck, the breath of more
than birth, more than death, beyond
your two great abilities. Different from cold,
harder to resist. He pads deliberately closer,
mouth wide, filled with stars.

This is the form in which he is most terrifying—
his pupil has opened so wide he can see
everything at once, just as it is, the sum of his will.
He will take what he chooses. You look as far
into his eye as you can bear, try to seem unafraid.
The dories lie open on the wharf, white bodies like
split shells. The cliffs darken until they cannot be seen.
This is not the god you dreamed of.

PATRICK WARNER
1963–

POEM WITHOUT BEGINNING OR END

because I can't see what's right before my
face, apparently: take how I barely noticed
the manner in which the faithful on their way
stopped beside that font, not only stopped
but how they dipped, and after dipping blessed:
what concerns me is their manner of blessing:

as gingerly is to reverently, as I extend
my fingers in this empty lunchtime lunchroom,
some dipped a hand inside as if to test
a hot iron, or the temperature of a bath,
then brought their glistening fingers up
to trace the line between forehead and chest,

then looped a stitch across the shoulders
left to right, or was it right to left—
I remember now, not having blessed myself
in years, I am certain—as it is a certainty
that repetition undermines certainty, try
signing one hundred travellers cheques

one after another; after a while all you'll
remember is the simple motion (a motion
you spent long pre-verbal years in learning),
the follow-me-motion of the magician
that conjures in its wake, as in the wake
of that slow motion blessing, an aura,

a grey-blue length of typewriter ribbon,
an eye-spot drawn out into an egg-timer
with one end missing; a primitive petroglyph
of a primitive fish; an optician's doodle;
a bow-tie glimpsed across a crowded room;
a serving table from the Bombay Company:

others, whether late or early, barely broke
their stride to dip, and, post-dipping, blessed
themselves offhandedly, as if dismissing
charity pleas or unsubstantiated claims,
as if shaking out a handkerchief, into which
there will be folded a commandeered wallet,

from which there will appear, transformed
(as I am changed by the magician's assistant—
my trousers make a tent when she bends over
to pick up the bird-cage and there appears
on the tips of the magician's outstretched
fingers) a fluttering dove, or albino pigeon:

the slowness of that movement's sleight of
hand, the magic of that movement taking form,
I would see later, as second or third hand,
at the hands of one ageing Pablo Picasso:
the artist captured on stills from a film
sketching the studio air with a blow-torch,

the fiery bull appearing and disappearing
as the master beholds the camera with eyes
so bald and passionate they might have been
my father's looking down the dinner table,
but giving no clue as to whether this airing
was some new kind of art or a forgery:

GUMSHOE

Packed in pick-up trucks they arrive at dawn,
these small, overalled, dark-skinned men,
from countries south of the Rio Grande,
who tend to the trees and bushes and lawns

in this mature suburban neighbourhood
where month-by-month nothing changes
except the flags, I mean the flags that flap
from slender dowels, that are set alongside

the tasselled poles that fly Old Glory,
silk flags set to mark a holiday or season,
pumpkins, shamrocks, hearts, and bunnies
signal the year-long consumer obsession,

in this neighbourhood where nobody walks,
where in places there are no sidewalks,
where no one seems to notice what I notice
when I walk, and there's no one to ask

about these inch-square zip-lock baggies
I find every morning, dew-fogged and stuck
to the pavement—what are these exactly,
sandwich bags for wee folk, for fairies?

Such folk myths belong to the old countries,
to the Irish pubs down by the harbour,
to Germanytowns, Dutchlands, Little Italies.
New World folklore is of a different order.

Myths here are a poor man's collateral,
so new they don't seem like myths at all,
but swap stocks and bonds for gold and silver
and the city skyline for the magic kingdom,

and you'll understand why these lawns
are tended each day by Guatemalans,
Mexicans, El Salvadorians, Peruvians,
and you'll know why yesterday when I found

a sanitary napkin perched on a gutter
my first thought was of a magic slipper,
followed by thoughts of the ugly sisters,
and girls who will cut off their toes to fit in,

because that's the way it is in this place,
where the bloated frog is always the prince,
where there is blind belief in tomorrow
and in the wealth tomorrow will bring.

Today it brought a pair of black underwear,
women's black Moschino underwear,
dropped in the middle of an intersection
where I barely had time to examine them.

I thought, naturally, of Puss 'n Boots,
and maybe because I knew the ogre's fate
something a bit more sinister crept in,
and, as well, I was getting these looks

from a pair of Mexicans or Guatemalans,
both of whose faces barely topped
the four-foot hedge they were trimming,
faces right off a frieze in Tenochtitlán.

What's next, I wondered, a severed finger,
an arm, a ripped-out human heart,
a dead co-ed like Snow White on a lawn
surrounded by seven diminutive men?

Not that I'm saying it's all going to happen,
(as cases go it's not open and shut),
there are reasons the future is hidden,
but clues, too, if you know how to look.

MORMON

How will a Mormon boy get a wife, I wondered,
if he declines his mission to wander the world,
spreading the Mormon word as he goes:
no wife for a Mormon boy who refuses.

So I was kind to two young Mormon men
who came to my door last Saturday morning—
the point man in short-sleeved shirt and blue tie,
his back-up in short-sleeved shirt and blue tie—

the former displaying a pulp magazine
which featured a story on the fashion industry
and its dangers, especially to young women:
anorexia, bulimia, and low self-esteem.

I listened until—as if at some prearranged signal—
the second flipped open a leather-bound book
he had held until then with a sloth-like grip.
It was my cue to say: I am not a Christian.

This has been true of my life for so long
that to say it out loud gives only a moderate high,
which in turn brings only a moderate low.
And so I did not take it too badly on coming back in

to hear my eight-year-old daughter say,
in her deepest voice: *I am not a Christian*;
though to hear her say it brought it home in a new way,
and I thought for a moment that this is serious

and that she should take it more seriously,
so I considered putting the fear into her, telling her
that if her grandfather heard her say such a thing
he would think us condemned to eternal damnation.

Instead, I sat back down on the couch beside her
where it so happened there was scheduled
an end-of-season *Fashion File*—the year's best show,
the year's best designer, the year's best newcomer.

And watching, I reserved my loudest cheers
for headdresses of ostrich and emu feathers,
for models with bleached invisible eyebrows,
for models with slack, stew-bone thighs.

While she preferred the more womanly models—
though she did not care for naked breasts—
and reserved her loudest cheers for young Marc Jacobs
and for the ready-to-wear from Donna Karan.

What a world this is for a Mormon boy, I thought,
who declines his mission to wander the world,
spreading the Mormon word as he goes:
what a world for a Mormon boy who refuses.

WATCHING THE OCEAN

You arrived that night in a shimmering slate-blue suit,
a linen rayon weave that still smelled of the factory,
and that, depending on how and where it rumpled,
showed a silver-whitish, semen, salt-lick sheen.

And all who dropped your name in conversation
as if they knew you, were suddenly quiet about it;
they could only watch how you moved from room
to room, restless in yourself but still at ease,

watch and wonder how—even as you grazed the buffet
for sea-salt chips and a foaming glass of 7UP—
you commanded such attention, reverence:
all felt in the presence of someone magnanimous.

But better from afar, you left each one you met
feeling smaller, undermined, like a bureaucrat
before sublimity, like a connoisseur of porn
reviewing videotapes of his daughter's delivery.

And even those who subscribed to the ideal,
who wished to be scoured of conceits, scattered
like crab claws, like lost bleach-bottle buoys
and massive main timbers on an isolated beach

found that they did not care for the experience.
Hence their tales of other nights and other parties,
of gale-force winds that blew without warning,
of houses left with not a stick unbroken.

THE TURN

On a steep hill, in a house for one
with a crooked cat and an antique bell,
in the middle of life. This is the place
where you made the turn, having crossed
the line where you could not tell
real from unreal, the climb from years,
wood from your flesh, fur from desire,
that silver bell from your tongue,
which tells the tale of that lonely time
when you thought you were ill,
thought you could not tell unreal
from real, your years from a hill,
self from a house, lust from a cat,
your talk from the sound of a bell.

THE MOLE

As though a hand had reached inside to rub
my liver. This was the nose of the mole.

Later, I felt a prickle, a draught in my eye.
This was the southwest breeze blowing
where the stone-blind mole had passed.

This was the meat of what was unspoken.
The absolute bedrock of morals, the top-soil
of incomprehension in which you turned
and said: Your wife tells me everything.

This was the unknown known, the mole
surfacing through the green. And blinking
by the swings on that suburban lawn
was my penchant for darkness and filth,
my penchant for sticking my nose in.

THE TOUCH TANK

The journeyman-welded crabs move stiffly
around inside the armour of their PhDs,
and with buck-stop stares contemplate attack.
Delicate flywheel motions near their mouths
suggest the nuanced exploration of this
thought: sideways-forward or sideways-back.

Nearby, artistic whelks confect ice-cream
dollop shells through which project soft
white sprouts of feeling, and extrude, below
their skeletons of fine Spode china, skirts of
same white flesh, houndstooth-flecked;
underneath, you know, they're all vagina.

A lead-foot shellfish revs, propels its bulk
along the bottom—its square hinge denotes
a scallop not a clam. Look! says someone,
pointing to an orange marble with a turban.
That, says the interpreter, is a sea peach,
and immediately ten little hands all reach.

Nearby, a pinkish bombed-out minaret
makes to the ear an age-old invitation,
until a hermit crab extends a clutch of claws.
Above, tumescent, slimy, warty and green,
a hoisted sea cucumber deftly shucks its
dildo status by pissing gently in the stream.

Who knew the inner life was this small
aquatic town, where a slightly wavering
whitish outline around everything suggests
a time before our principles took hold,
before the whore's egg spawned a crown,
before a maimed starfish jigged cruciform.

WAXING

It began when I hit the snooze and slept in late,
        got worse when I perched on the edge of the bed
and in one fluid motion attempted to pull
        my still fastened shirt down over my head.

It was that kind of morning, a broken button
        I had once thought neat as a crescent moon
lodged with force on the bridge of my nose
        and cut into my flesh, a sickle. Blood trickled,

dripped from my nose to my lip to my lap,
        thereby waking a sleeper cell
in the form of a newly cut key which the guy
        at the key shop hadn't properly sanded.

In no time at all it turned into a breadknife,
        quietly sawing a hole in my pocket,
unbeknownst to me until the moment I reached
        for the gas pump and felt the spill

of coins down my leg. One lodged in my shoe,
        while several more scattered out in the slush
where they seemed to refresh themselves,
        turned silvery in the pavement's salted wet.

Like sparrows around a heated bird bath
        those coins seemed—if I can say such a thing—
to be enjoying themselves, seemed to be saying
        that every cloud has a nickel-alloy lining.

They said ignore the fact that bad things
        always happen in threes. Look up, they said,
and there above the park I saw a falcate moon,
        and felt again the pull of mysterious forces,

the magnetic coming together of pieces
          in a meaningless meaningful way—Professor,
let me explain: it's where the rule of three
          meets Murphy's law, it's the moment when

the number of things the average mind can recall
          is exceeded by one, but the spirit drawing
on unstable power—not Strong-Cobb units of force,
          but Olivia Newton Joules of laughter—

invents an on-the-spot order. And so it was
          I took in the grin of that cracked-Aspirin moon
aligned above the bust of Winston Churchill,
          an unusual bust sawn off at the nipples,

and placed on a chest-high plinth in the
          eponymous park in such a way
that it looks as though he has stepped behind
          that polished granite block to take a piss,

his bulldog scowl revealing not only his
          bloody-mindedness but perhaps a waxing trouble
with his flow, much like that pump clocking
          five cents at a time in the early morning ten below.

ANOREXIA

The less there is of you the more of me.
The doctors refer to me as he.
He is not you, they say to her.
She takes a shaky breath. She runs around
and I run with her underground.

I play my hostess like a violin,
my minimalist concerto for torso and limbs.
That's you in the loo, your woodwind guts,
the cymbal splash of watery vomit,
the kettledrum of bowels in the bowl.

I am the heart of these stick figures,
don't bother asking where I come from.
Look to the weak strain in your code.
Look to notions of perfection,
to where you fall short in execution.

My hostess dreams of becoming an actress,
dreams of the lead in *Les Mis*.
She gives me such a deep and hungry kiss;
she'll end up in the hospital next to the hospice,
where I may have to tighten my belt.

She imagines a memorial Mass in Maine:
the mourners arrive by private plane
and are ferried to the church in limousines.
I play the mourners like a violin,
my catgut bow weeping and wailing.

I spend most of my time not dying.
They spend most of their time trying.
Those last two I plucked from Fred Seidel.
I could go on, in fact, I think I will,
my passion for girl flesh is inexhaustible.

Tuesdays we meet with her group—
the Boa-restrictors, my own little cult.
One has a ribcage like a catcher's mitt
One takes pills to make her shit.
One shaves lanugo off her limbs.

Clouds cluster and turn the sky purple.
Little children splash about in puddles.
A Pomeranian takes on a Bichon Frise.
My little pets are down on their knees.
The less there is of you the more of me.

I spend most of my time not dying.
They spend most of their time trying.
I am the Caesar of their seizures. They are the kill.
I'm at the heart of these stick figures' hearts.
I could go on. I could stop. I will.

THE THERAPIST

In just five minutes she gave us our narratives:
you were the smoother-over, the peacemaker,
while I was the perfectionist, and together
we had passed these traits to our daughter,
given her food for her eating disorder.

"Do you want to be right or be happy?"
she asked. "That's too simple," I said,
"it doesn't need to be one or the other.
I feel happy when I'm right and right
when I'm happy. They can go together."

In just five minutes she gave us our narratives:
you were the smoother-over, the peacemaker,
while I was the perfectionist, and together
we had passed these traits to our daughter,
given her food for her eating disorder.

This was the pattern to be broken,
the second nature that usurped our natures,
but only if we admitted the problem:
that was fifty percent of the cure, the rest
would come from time in her care.

"Do you want to be right or be happy?"
Who doesn't want to be happy all the time?
Who doesn't want to believe in that fable?
She said she could fit us with flexible tools,
I thought about hardware. We nodded like fools.

In just five minutes she gave us our narratives:
you were the smoother-over, the peacemaker,
while I was the perfectionist, and together
we had passed these traits to our daughter,
given her food for her eating disorder.

She told us we each had the power to choose
not to let others take over our lives,
then she covered herself by means of disclosure:
"I myself was something of a perfectionist.
I myself was the great smoother-over."

This was the pattern to be broken,
the second nature that usurped our natures,
but only if we admitted the problem.
She showed us the root and solution.
I squirmed in my seat, a retrograde symptom.

"Imagine you're old," she said, "at sixty-five.
What then will you think about having been angry
for the best years of your children's lives?"
I nodded my head while plotting murder,
"I'll do anything," I said, "to help my daughter."

A HISTORY OF THE LOMBARDS

for Carmine Starnino

i

Because I no longer trust my eyes, I can tell you about the Lombards,
    who not only hauled their huts on sleds from the frozen reindeer lands,
but also brought the frontier with them, presenting it to their enemies,
    the settled-down folk, the soft and comfortable, the easily fooled.

The further south the Lombards went the more gullible the people.
    How else to explain the deception carried by the Lombard women,
who in beards woven from their tresses stood disguised as men
    among their men, a shadow army, flickering between campfires?

Ahead of the Lombard advance ran rumours of dog-headed soldiers
    who ate nothing but blood-soaked oats, and would, if kept from battle,
gut themselves so as to gorge on their own gore. In this way, whole armies
    weakened and were broken before the fighting even began.

ii

The Lombard king, by this time half-blind, halted one evening
    his piebald mare so she could drink her fill from a fish pond,
but what he saw there made him stare for some time, made him twirl
    his birch lance and with its butt end stir the waters,

what he saw filled his heart not with fear but admiration
    and gratitude for a life that could still move him to wonder.
Long he squinted into the brackish, leaf-flecked pool where squirmed
    seven infants, his attention undisturbed by the laughs and advances

of the prostitute who had just that morning delivered them,
    the spell broken only when a fat fist gripped the ladling spear
and the old king, seized and shaking, raised from the fish pond
    a banner: his streaming, wriggling, blue-eyed successor.

The day the Lombards faced the Heroli the sky divided. Above
    the Lombards it brooded while above their enemy it remained blue.
Both camps read this as an omen. It was clear to all there would be
    a decisive victory. Dear reader, can you tell me which side won?

I guessed—from that blue sky—the Heroli, but I was wrong.
    Who knew that a spell brewed in the Lombard's cloud boil?
Soon thunderhead hammers fell on their enemy, so confusing them
    they mistook the green flax fields at their backs as pools

fit for swimming, and reaching out arms and kicking out legs
    tried to breaststroke. This was how the Lombards found them,
dazed creatures thrashing a foreign element, defenceless babes,
    carp in a well, easily caught, easily speared, easily killed.

ACKNOWLEDGEMENTS

KEN BABSTOCK: "Camping at Glendalough" and "Finishing," *Mean* (Anansi, 1999); "Carrying someone else's infant past a cow in a field near Marmora, Ont.," "The 7-Eleven Formerly Known as Rx," and "Tractor," *Days into Flatspin* (Anansi, 2001); "Pragmatist," "The Minds of the Higher Animals," "Materialist," and "Compatibilist," *Airstream Land Yacht* (Anansi, 2006); and "As Marginalia in John Clare's *The Rural Muse*" and "Methodist Hatchet," *Methodist Hatchet* (Anansi, 2011), are reprinted by permission of House of Anansi Press, Toronto.

MICHAEL CRUMMEY: "Old Wives' Tales," "Kite," and "Newfoundland Sealing Disaster," *Hard Light* (Brick, 1998), are reprinted by permission of the author. "The Late Macbeth," "Artifacts," and "The Naked Man," excerpted from *Salvage* by Michael Crummey. Copyright © 2002 Michael Crummey. Reprinted by permission of McClelland & Stewart. "Under the Keel," "The Selected," "Boys," "Girls," "Fox on the Funk Islands," and "Datsun," *Under the Keel* (Anansi, 2013), are reprinted by permission of House of Anansi Press, Toronto. "Keel" is printed by permission of the author.

MARY DALTON: "Bridesboys," "The Cross-handed Bed," "The Doctor," "Down the Bay," "First Boat," "Janneying," "Merrybegot," "The Ragged Jacket," "Winter Coal," and "Yet," *Merrybegot* (Signal, 2003); and "Salax," "The Salt Man," "Osmotic," and "The Boat," *Red Ledger* (Signal, 2006) are reprinted by permission of Signal Editions, Véhicule Press.

TOM DAWE: "Babel," *Hemlock Cove and After* (Breakwater, 1975), is reprinted by permission of the author. "A Fairy Tale," "Outport Christmas," "Abandoned Outport," "Evening, Bareneed, Conception Bay," "Top of the World," "Edwardians (Old Photograph)," "Wild Geese," "If Sonnets Were in Fashion," and "Alders," *In Hardy Country* (Breakwater, 1993); and "Bess," "New Year's Morning, 2000," and "The Last House," *Where Genesis Begins* (Breakwater, 2009) are reprinted by permission of Breakwater Books.

RICHARD GREENE: "On Sherbourne Street," "At the College," and "Beside the Funeral Home," "Apparitions," "1000X," "Custom," "Whaler," "The White Fleet," and "Crossing the Straits," *Boxing the Compass* (Signal, 2009), are reprinted by permission of the author.

been 300 Pounds," and "Percy Janes Boarding the Bus," *In the Old Country of My Heart* (Killick, 1996), are reprinted by permission of the author. "I Solemn," "The Laying Out, 1956," and "Storm," *Going Around with Bachelors* (Brick, 2007), are reprinted by permission of the author.

PATRICK WARNER: "Poem Without Beginning or End," *All Manner of Misunderstanding* (Killick, 2001), is reprinted by permission of Killick Press. "Gumshoe," "Mormon," and "Watching the Ocean," *There, There* (Signal, 2005), are reprinted by permission of Véhicule Press. "The Turn," "The Mole," and "The Touch Tank," *Mole* (Anansi, 2009), are used by permission of House of Anansi Press, Toronto. "Waxing," "Anorexia," "The Therapist," and "A History of the Lombards," originally published by Goose Lane Editions in *Perfection*, copyright © 2012 by Patrick Warner, are used by permission of Goose Lane Editions.

THE EXCERPT from E.J. Pratt's obituary, used in the prologue, was originally published by *The Times* (London) on April 28, 1964, and is reprinted by permission of *The Times* / NI Syndication.

MICHAEL PITTMAN'S cover image, "Ignis," mixed media on panel, 2008, is printed by permission of the Canadian Artists Representation Copyright Collective.

MARK CALLANAN gratefully acknowledges the support of the City of St. John's Arts Jury and the Access Copyright Foundation's Research Grant program for financial support while researching this anthology.

CONTRIBUTORS

KEN BABSTOCK was born in Burin, Placentia Bay, and raised in the Ottawa Valley. He has published four collections of poetry: *Mean* (1999), *Days into Flatspin* (2001), *Airstream Land Yacht* (2006), and *Methodist Hatchet* (2011), which won the 2012 Griffin Poetry Prize. He lives in Toronto.

MICHAEL CRUMMEY was born in Buchans. He has published four collections of poetry: *Arguments with Gravity* (1996), *Hard Light* (1998), *Salvage* (2002), and *Under the Keel* (2013). As a novelist, Crummey's work has been shortlisted for the Giller Prize. He lives in St. John's.

MARY DALTON was born in Lake View, Conception Bay. She has published five collections of poetry: *The Time of Icicles* (1989), *Allowing the Light* (1993), *Merrybegot* (2003), which won the 2004 E.J. Pratt Poetry Award, *Red Ledger* (2006), and *Hooking* (2013). She lives in St. John's.

TOM DAWE was born in Long Pond, Manuels, Conception Bay. He has published four collections of poetry: *Hemlock Cove and After* (1975), *Island Spell* (1981), *In Hardy Country* (1993), and *Where Genesis Begins* (2009). Currently the Poet Laureate for the city of St. John's, Dawe received the Order of Canada in 2011. He lives in Conception Bay South.

RICHARD GREENE was born in St. John's. He has published three collections of poetry: *Republic of Solitude* (1994), *Crossing the Straits* (2004), and *Boxing the Compass* (2009), which won the 2010 Governor General's Award for Poetry. He lives in Cobourg, Ontario.

CARMELITA MCGRATH was born in Branch, St. Mary's Bay. She has published three collections of poetry: *Poems on Land and Water* (1992), *To the New World* (1997), which won the 1998 Atlantic Poetry Prize, and *Escape Velocity* (2013). She lives in St. John's.

AL PITTMAN: was born in St. Leonard's, Placentia Bay. He published six collections of poetry before his death in 2001: *The Elusive Resurrection* (1966), *Seaweed and Rosaries* (1968), *Through One More Window* (1974), *Once When I was Drowning* (1978), *Dancing in Limbo* (1993), and *Thirty-for-Sixty* (1999). A selected poems, *Island in the Sky*, appeared posthumously in 2003; his collected poems will be published by Breakwater in 2013.

SUE SINCLAIR was born in Guelph, Ontario and raised in St. John's. She has published four collections of poetry: *Secrets of Weather and Hope* (2001), *Mortal Arguments* (2003), *The Drunken Lovely Bird* (2005), which won the 2005 Independent Publisher's Poetry Award, and *Breaker* (2008). She lives in Montreal.

JOHN STEFFLER was born in Toronto and moved to Corner Brook in 1975. He has published six collections of poetry: *An Explanation of Yellow* (1981), *The Grey Islands* (1985), *The Wreckage of Play* (1988), *That Night We Were Ravenous* (1998), *Helix: New and Selected Poems* (2002), and *Lookout* (2010), which was shortlisted for the Griffin Poetry Prize. Steffler is a former Canadian Poet Laureate. He lives in Maberly, Ontario.

AGNES WALSH was born in Placentia, Placentia Bay. She has published two collections of poetry: *In The Old Country of My Heart* (1996) and *Going Around with Bachelors* (2007). She is a former Poet Laureate for the city of St. John's. She lives in St. John's.

PATRICK WARNER was born in Claremorris, Co. Mayo, Ireland, and moved to St. John's in 1980. He has published four collections of poetry: *All Manner of Misunderstanding* (2001), *There, There* (2005), *Mole* (2009), and *Perfection* (2012). He is a two-time winner of the E.J. Pratt Poetry Award and lives in St. John's.

INDEX OF TITLES

www.ingramcontent.com/pod-product-compliance
Lightning Source LLC
Chambersburg PA
CBHW031252090426
42742CB00007B/414